In Context

Functional Skills English

ENTRY 3 – LEVEL 2

 Motor Vehicle Technology Workbook

D1331028

John Meed
Anna Rossetti

 Nelson Thornes

This edition published in 2013 by:
Nelson Thornes Ltd
Delta Place
27 Bath Road
CHELTENHAM
GL53 7TH
United Kingdom

13 14 15 16 17 / 10 9 8 7 6 5 4 3 2 1

A catalogue record for this book is available from the British Library

ISBN 978 1 4085 1834 2

Cover image: Kudryashka/Shutterstock

Illustrations by James Elston and Paul McCaffrey, Sylvie Poggio Agency

Page make-up by Pantek Media, Maidstone

Printed in China

Acknowledgements
The authors and the publisher would like to thank the following for permission to reproduce material:

Text
p5 © The Triumph Sports Six Club 2012; pp9, 11 from Health and Safety Executive © Crown Copyright 2012; p18 'Buying an MPV:
as easy as ABC' published by the Warwick Courier, 12 April 2012. All rights reserved © 2012, Johnston Publishing Limited; p34
© 2012 MCL Ltd; p38 Copyright © 2012 Northcliffe Media Limited. All rights reserved; p54 reviews from Parkers.co.uk © Bauer
Media 2012; p58 © Next Green Car Ltd 2008–2012; p68 'What does the computer in a car do?' Copyright © 1998–2012
HowStuffWorks, Inc; p84 car advertisements from trade-it.co.uk; p94 Institute of Advanced Motorists © 2011; p104 from direct.gov.uk
© Crown Copyright, 2012; p114 © 2012 BoostTown.com; p118 Copyright © Wales Rally GB, 2012.

Images
p5 © PJF/Alamy, p8 info from author, p9 © a la france/Alamy, p14 © Radius Images/Alamy, p15 Volvo Car UK Ltd, p18 VW, p27
© Oredia/Alamy, p28 © Andrew Spiers/Alamy, p38 © imagebroker/Alamy, p48 © IS2 from Image source/Alamy, p54 © Motoring
Picture Library/Alamy, p54 Ford Motor Company Ltd, p54 © P Cox/Alamy, p54 © Robert Steinbarth/Alamy, p58 Toyota, p64
© Image Source/Alamy, p68 VW, p68 © Brian Jackson, p78 Ford Motor Company Ltd, p84 © Phil Talbot/Alamy, p84 © Trinity
Mirror/Mirrorpix/Alamy, p84 © simon clay/Alamy, p88 © Design Pics Inc./Alamy, p108 George Williams/Toyota, p114 Skalapendra,
p116 Maxim Blinkov, p118 © Robert Pitman/Alamy, p118 © Action Plus Sports Images/Alamy

Every effort has been made to trace the copyright holders but if any have been inadvertently overlooked the publisher will be
pleased to make the necessary arrangements at the first opportunity.

Contents

Introduction

"Functional skills are the fundamental, applied skills in English, mathematics, and information and communication technology (ICT) which help people to gain the most from life, learning and work."

Ofqual (2012), Criteria for Functional Skills Qualifications

This workbook is designed to present functional English in a variety of contexts to make it accessible and relevant to you, as Motor Vehicle Technology candidates. It is intended to be written in, so use it as a record of your progress!

Being 'functional' means that you will:

- be able to apply skills to all sorts of real-life contexts

- have the mental ability to take on challenges in a range of new settings

- be able to work independently

- realise that tasks often need persistence, thought and reflection.

Features of this workbook are:

 **Source**

These pages will cover important aspects of Motor Vehicle Technology and consist of some interesting source materials, such as newspaper articles or industry-related information, followed by various questions and activities for you to complete.

 **FOCUS ON**

Each Focus on is 2 pages long and will teach you specific Functional Skills. They include:

- guidance on the skill

- one or more activities to practise the skill.

Good luck!

The Triumph Sports Six Club

In 1959 Triumph Cars introduced a new small family car – the Herald. The design of the chassis made it easy to produce a number of other cars with different body styles and engines. These included a more sporty saloon and convertible, the Vitesse, and two outright sports cars, the Spitfire and GT6.

These are now known as 'classic cars', which is the description for any car manufactured from around 1945 to 1980. If the car was registered before 1972, the owner doesn't have to pay car tax on it.

When production of all of these Triumphs ceased in the late 1970s a group of enthusiasts formed the Triumph Sports Six Club (TSSC) in an effort to keep as many of these well-loved cars as possible on the road. The club produces a regular magazine for members called the *Courier*. A recent editorial announced a plan to encourage more young people to join the club.

Here's what the editor wrote.

Let's encourage the young people

It has long been an aim of the TSSC to encourage more young people to get involved with Triumphs and become a part of our great Club. So let's take a look at what is happening.

First, we've been looking at how to make Club membership more affordable to young members.

With this in mind, it has been proposed that we introduce a discounted membership fee for all 17–21-year-olds who wish to join the TSSC. This is a very positive move to attract young people to the Club and to our wonderful hobby.

I would like to tell you about TSSC member Aaron Brown. Aaron is 17 and has recently passed his driving test.

His very first car is a Spitfire 1500 and he's on the road with a little help from the TSSC and our Insurance Panel, where he was able to get insurance cover at a rate that compared very favourably with the cost of insuring a small modern hatchback.

Those of you who frequent the Message Board on the website will know that Aaron's car is unfortunately suffering from some serious-sounding engine problems and may need a rebuild. It's great to see all the help and advice being offered by more experienced members, and he is also able to call the Club Technical Helpline for advice. If we, the experienced Triumph enthusiasts, rally round and support young people like Aaron, with luck, we can start them on a lifetime of fun with Triumphs. We all know how rewarding that can be.

A Read the text and answer the questions.

1 Which Triumph car provided the basis for the chassis design of a range of others?
   a) Vitesse
   b) Spitfire
   c) Herald

2 What is the name of the magazine of the Triumph Sports Six Club?
   a) *It's a Triumph!*
   b) *Courier*
   c) *Club Car*

3 Which car has Aaron bought?
   a) Spitfire 1500
   b) Triumph GT6
   c) Spitfire Mark 3

4 How would readers know that Aaron's car has engine problems?
   a) Through the Technical Helpline
   b) From the TSSC website
   c) From talking to other owners

5 What kind of car are Spitfires and Triumph GT6s ?
   a) Convertibles
   b) Vintage cars
   c) Classic cars

6 Where did Aaron get advice on insurance?
   a) From the TSSC Insurance Panel
   b) From the *Courier* magazine
   c) From TSSC members

B Read the text and answer the questions.

1 Who is likely to read this magazine?

2 What kind of person wrote the editorial and do you think they are young or older? Give reasons for your answer.

C The article says that Aaron was 'able to get insurance cover at a rate that compared very favourably with the cost of insuring a small modern hatchback'.

1 What does the writer mean by this?

2 Think about the following points and make notes about your opinions before discussing them in a small group.

- Did you know that it often costs less to insure a classic car?
- Why is this the case?
- Do you think insurance premiums for young people are fair?
- What do you think about male and female drivers paying the same rate of insurance?

   Write your notes here.

D Choose a word from the list below to fill the gaps in the sentences that follow.

registered   wonderful   enthusiasts   experienced   manufactured

1 A car [   ] from around 1945 to 1980 is known as a 'classic car'.

2 If your car was [   ] before 1972, you do not have to pay car tax.

E Match each word to its definition.

Word	Definition
1 Affordable	a) someone who is very interested in a particular hobby
2 Enthusiast	b) when the price of something has been reduced by a particular amount
3 Discounted	c) reasonably priced

3   Aaron is getting a lot of help and advice from [   ] members of the TSSC.

4   The TSSC was set up by a group of Triumph [   ].

5   Owning and looking after a Triumph sports car is a [   ] hobby.

F   Which of these statements are presented in the text as fact and which are presented as opinion?

1   The TSSC has a plan to encourage young people to join the Club.   Fact ◯   Opinion ◯

2   Aaron's car is suffering from some engine problems that sound serious.   Fact ◯   Opinion ◯

3   Aaron is likely to have a lifetime of fun with Triumphs.   Fact ◯   Opinion ◯

4   The discounted membership fee is a very positive move.   Fact ◯   Opinion ◯

G   Write a list of reasons why people might enjoy owning a classic car.

People would enjoy owning a classic car because:

Discuss your list with a partner.
Did you have the same reasons?

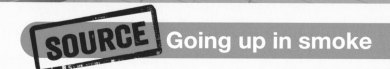

Fire and explosion

Fires and explosions are the cause of most deaths and property damage in motor vehicle repair (MVR). Most result from mishandling petrol when draining fuel tanks and lines, but others happen during 'hot work' (any process that generates flames, sparks or heat), repairs on diesel tanks, or the inappropriate use of paints and thinners.

As well as fuel, other flammable substances used in MVR include waste engine oil, paints, solvents, cleaning materials, fibreglass and aerosols. There are also risks when working with airbags and equipment used for battery charging, welding or cutting.

Make sure you use safe methods of work with flammable materials and high temperatures. Here are some dos and don'ts:

- Do use a fuel retriever/adaptor when draining petrol from tanks and lines.
- Do store containers of flammable liquids in a designated fire proof cupboard.
- Before carrying out any 'hot work' on drums or other containers that may contain vapours such as petrol, diesel, paints, solvents, etc., do carefully consider the risks. Safer options include using cold cutting techniques and replacing rather than repairing them.
- Where hot work on a tank or drum is necessary, do reduce the risks by emptying and cleaning it and making sure any gas is safe.
- Do not drain petrol over or close to pits or drains.

- Do not smoke, weld or carry out other hot work while handling petrol or flammable paints and thinners.
- Do not use petrol or thinners to burn rubbish or unwanted materials.

The Dangerous Substances and Explosive Atmospheres Regulations 2002 (DSEAR) require employers to:

- find out what dangerous substances are in their workplace and what the fire and explosion risks are
- put control measures in place to remove risks or to control them
- take steps to reduce the effects of any incidents
- prepare plans and procedures to deal with accidents, incidents and emergencies
- inform and train employees about the risks from fire and explosions
- identify areas where explosive atmospheres may occur and avoid ignition sources in these areas.

A Match each word to its definition.

Word	Definition
1 Inappropriate	a) the chance of something going wrong
2 Flammable	b) handling something in the wrong way
3 Mishandling	c) something that can burn
4 Risk	d) starting a fire
5 Ignition	e) not suitable

B True or false?

Which of these statements are true and which are false, according to the text?

1 Most fires and explosions result from mishandling petrol when draining fuel tanks and lines.　　True ◯　　False ◯

2 It is safe to drain petrol into drains.　　True ◯　　False ◯

3 Flammable substances include waste engine oil, paints, solvents and cleaning materials.　　True ◯　　False ◯

4 Hot work is any process that generates flames, sparks or heat.　　True ◯　　False ◯

C Write down answers to these questions.

1 Who is this text written for?

2 What is the purpose of the text?

3 Give two examples of flammable substances found in a workshop.

a)

b)

4 Give two examples of things you should not do.

a)

b)

5 What does the law say employers must find out?

D Read this real case study.

> A motor mechanic removed the fuel gauge sender unit from a fuel tank and started to drain the petrol into a bucket. There was more petrol in the tank than he thought and it spilled onto the floor and caught fire. The mechanic suffered severe burns to hands, arms and legs and the workshop was completely destroyed.

E With a partner, discuss these questions.

• Were you aware of the risks of fire and explosions?

• Have you heard about any similar incidents in garages?

• Have you ever felt in danger?

F How well did you and your partner listen to each other? Give yourselves a score for each statement below.

• Score 3 if this was true most of the time.

• Score 2 if this was sometimes true.

• Score 1 if this did not happen very often.

Statement	Score (1–3)
We took turns to speak.	
We listened carefully when the other person spoke.	
We looked at each other often while we were talking.	
We avoided interrupting each other.	
We showed when we agreed, e.g. by nodding, saying 'yes'.	
We asked questions to check we had understood.	

G Write down two things that you could do another time to make sure you listen to each other carefully.

1

2

H Write a checklist of ways in which you can reduce the risk of fire and explosion in a garage.

FOCUS ON Proper nouns

Sentences start with a capital letter, but capital letters are also used for proper nouns. These are the names of a specific or unique:

- person
- place
- organisation
- item or brand.

Days of the week and months also have capitals (e.g. Monday, July), as do titles, such as Mr, Mrs and Ms.

Proper nouns are different from common nouns, which do not have capitals.

Here are some examples:

Common noun	Proper noun
person	Ms Ayisha Khan
city	Bristol
country	France
garage	Formula One Autocentre
organisation	Automobile Association
car	Mercedes
place	Silverstone

 A Four of these words are proper nouns. Which ones are they?

- Kevin
- Temperature
- Visitor
- Oxford
- Hazard
- Peugeot
- Differential
- Michelin

B The sentences below have no capital letters in them. Underline each word that should start with a capital letter.

1 mr paul stevens is the manager of green hill motors.

2 julie is a sales assistant and works on friday, saturday and sunday.

3 the car was insured with aviva.

4 mark will take his holiday in july.

5 the institute of the motor industry is based in london.

6 there are more than 500 car component suppliers in birmingham.

7 peter took the citroën out for a test drive.

8 the lunch menu gave a choice of roast chicken or macaroni cheese.

9 the royal automobile club is a national motoring association.

10 the sales team ate at pizza express.

C Give an example of a proper noun for each category in the list below.

1 Town

2 Equipment

4 Brand

5 Person

6 Place

Blind spot detection systems in 25 per cent of new cars by 2016

Blind spot detection (BSD) systems first began to appear in top-of-the-line consumer vehicles around 2005, with Volvo leading the way. By 2011, such systems were available on high-volume models such as the Ford Focus and Mercedes-Benz C-Class. By 2016, ABI Research forecast that annual BSD installations will reach 20 million (just over 25 per cent of the predicted world vehicle market), with a worldwide market value of over £7.5 bn.

'Blind spot detection has struggled for recognition in its early days as a standalone application,' says principal analyst David Alexander, 'perhaps because it has been unfairly classified as a feature for less-competent drivers. But the feature is becoming more popular because it's now better understood that the experienced driver can switch on the indicator to carry out an extra check before changing lanes.'

More recently, with the introduction of radar-based systems, additional functionality has made the BSD option even more attractive. The emergence of cross-traffic alert is probably the most significant event, because it offers the driver information about local traffic that is not available elsewhere.

'Another enhancement to the blind spot monitoring feature is lane change assist', says research director Larry Fisher. 'This feature uses the sensors to check for approaching vehicles up to 50 m behind as well as making sure there is no obstacle in the blind spot. An extra warning is given to the driver when they switch on the indicator lights and another vehicle is either already overtaking or approaching rapidly.'

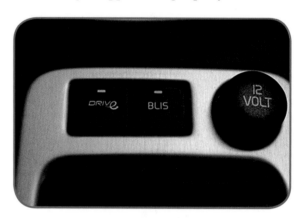

BSD can also be linked to lane-keeping systems that can provide steering or individual wheel braking to help the driver stay in lane. Many manufacturers are starting to integrate the two systems together, which means that drivers get electronic 'machine vision' to help them stay in lane and be safer when deciding to move out of the current lane.

A What is the main purpose of the text 'Blind spot detection systems in 25 per cent of new cars by 2016'?

B According to the text, what proportion of new cars are likely to have BSD systems by 2016?

1 A quarter ⃝

2 Almost a half ⃝

3 Just over a quarter ⃝

4 Almost three quarters ⃝

C According to the text, when were BSD systems first introduced in high-volume cars?

1 2005 ⃝

2 2009 ⃝

3 2011 ⃝

4 2016 ⃝

D According to the text, which one of these statements is true?

1 BSD systems are for less-competent drivers. ⃝

2 BSD systems were first introduced for cheaper cars. ⃝

3 BSD systems check for obstacles in the blind spot. ⃝

4 BSD systems provide steering or individual wheel braking. ⃝

E According to the text, identify two other applications that may be linked to BSD.

1

2

F Which of these statements are presented in the text as fact and which as opinion?

1 BSD systems first began to appear in top-of-the-line consumer vehicles.   Fact ⃝   Opinion ⃝

2 Blind spot detection has struggled for recognition.   Fact ⃝   Opinion ⃝

3　BSD has been classified as a feature for less-competent drivers.　　Fact ◯　　Opinion ◯

4　A driver can switch on the indicator to carry out an extra check before changing lanes.　　Fact ◯　　Opinion ◯

G　In a small group, discuss these issues.

1　Have you noticed a blind spot in cars that you or other people have driven?

[ ]

2　What problems can a blind spot cause?

[ ]

3　Would you value having a BSD system in your car?

[ ]

H　Choose a word from the list below to fill the gaps in the sentences that follow.

　　vehicle　　linked　　light　　motorways　　detection　　data

Blind spot [ ] systems typically have two small radars hidden in the rear bumper. The radars detect any [ ] moving beside or behind the car. A computer combines the [ ] from the two radars and this is communicated to the driver, usually by a [ ] coming on. The system works both on [ ] and in towns. BSD systems can be [ ] to lane-keeping systems.

I　Write two paragraphs about an application for vehicles that you know about.

　　Describe the main features of the application:

　　Describe what benefits the application has for drivers:

MPV – as easy as ABC

If you are thinking of buying an MPV, think carefully and make sure you choose the one that is right for you. Here is some straightforward information about the different types of MPV to get you started.

MPV stands for multi-purpose vehicle – one that gives maximum flexibility for seating arrangements and load-carrying options. Essentially, there are three basic types of MPV today.

A – Small cars with big ideas

First up are supermini-based models, developed from shopping runabouts such as the Toyota Yaris or the Mitsubishi Colt. These are basically small cars with big ideas. After all, just because you need a little car, there is no reason why it cannot be almost as versatile as a bigger one. These vehicles will not carry more people than a standard car, but they do offer much more flexible accommodation. This type also includes small van-based MPVs such as the Renault Kangoo and Citroën Berlingo Multispace.

When the supermini MPV is well designed the results can be truly impressive. An example is Vauxhall's Meriva. Here is a car that is not much longer than a Fiesta but has more interior space than a much larger mini-MPV such as the Renault Scénic. If you fold all of the seats down there is more luggage space than in a Mercedes E-class executive saloon. Keep all of the seats up and you have just about enough room for a family of five – for a lot less money than the cheapest Astra or Focus.

B – The family car

The next level of mini-MPV includes cars such as the Renault Scénic and the Citroën C4 Picasso. These are all based on family hatchbacks such as the Megane, Citroën C4 and Astra. In nearly all models you are still restricted to the same five-seater carrying capacity that you would find in an ordinary family hatchback. But then, the designers reckon it is not the number of seats you have, it is what you can do with them that counts.

C – The big beasts

Finally, there are the larger cars that you tend to picture when someone says 'MPV'. The Ford Galaxy and its clones, the VW Sharan and SEAT Alhambra lead this market, followed by the Peugeot 807, which can usually carry the driver and six passengers. All right, so large MPVs are a little van-like (OK, very van-like), but if you are a parent with two or three children and perhaps a dog, then their charms are hard to ignore, especially when you consider the amount of stuff you tend to have to carry on almost every journey.

So, think carefully about your real needs before you go shopping for an MPV. You might end up deciding you do not really need one at all. If you are tempted, however, try plenty of different types before you choose – and take the family to the showroom with you.

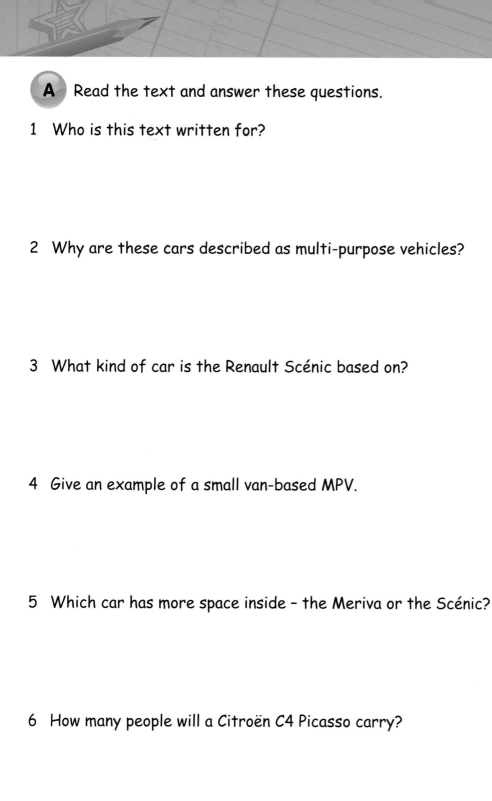

A Read the text and answer these questions.

1 Who is this text written for?

2 Why are these cars described as multi-purpose vehicles?

3 What kind of car is the Renault Scénic based on?

4 Give an example of a small van-based MPV.

5 Which car has more space inside – the Meriva or the Scénic?

6 How many people will a Citroën C4 Picasso carry?

7 Give one example of a large MPV.

8 What should you do before you decide on an MPV?

B Match each word to its definition.

Word	Definition
1 Flexibility	a) something that is a copy of a product from another manufacturer
2 Versatile	b) the amount that can be contained in something
3 Capacity	c) the ability to change or be changed according to circumstances
4 Clone	d) can be used for different purposes

C Write the name of the manufacturer of each of these cars.

1 ⬚ Kangoo

2 ⬚ Meriva

3 ⬚ C4 Picasso

4 ⬚ Galaxy

5 ⬚ Alhambra

6 ⬚ Yaris

D Which MPV?

Choose the best type of MPV for these people. Give reasons for your choices.

> Dave and Sandra have four children. They live in the centre of town where it is hard to park. The car is used mainly by Sandra to take the children to their friends' houses, school or activities. The family needs a car that will also be suitable for long drives when they go on holiday when they take Granny with them.

> Anya is a florist. She makes flower arrangements at home and delivers them to customers in the local area. She needs a vehicle that is nippy and makes it easy for her to get around, but can also accommodate her floral arrangements, which are sometimes quite large.

> India and Mario have just got married. She is about to sell her car as she gets a bus to work and does not need it any more. They are planning to trade in Mario's Ford Focus for an MPV. They like going walking in the country and camping and want something that will take all of their gear.

In your group, discuss what each of you has written. Be prepared to make a case for your top factors.

1   Which type of MPV is best for Dave and Sandra?

Why?

2   Which type of MPV is best for Anya?

Why?

3   Which type of MPV is best for India and Mario?

Why?

E Think about which factors you would take into account if you were choosing an MPV, such as make, reliability, power, appearance.
Choose your top five and put them in order of importance.

1

2

3

4

5

FOCUS ON Apostrophes

There are two ways in which we use apostrophes:

- When letters are missing
- To show possession

Apostrophes to show that letters are missing

When we deliberately shorten a word or phrase we can use an apostrophe to show that letters are missing. This is also called a 'contraction'.

We use an apostrophe when two words are combined to make one

- For example: 'I am' is shortened to 'I'm'.

A Replace the words in brackets with one word containing an apostrophe.

1 (He is) [_____] changing the pollen filter.

2 We can't do the service until next week because (we are) [_____] busy.

3 (They are) [_____] bringing in the car for repair on Tuesday.

We often use an apostrophe to replace 'have' or 'has'

- For example: 'we have' is shortened to 'we've'.

B Replace the words in brackets with one word containing an apostrophe.

1 (I have) [_____] finished the oil change.

2 (They have) [_____] booked a service next week.

3 Dave has given me a leaflet (he has) [_____] written about tyres.

The word 'not' is often shortened to 'n't'

- For example: 'is not' is shortened to 'isn't'.

C Replace the words in brackets with one word containing an apostrophe.

1 Ben (was not) [_____] able to come to work today.

2 We (were not) [_____] expecting the delivery.

3 We (cannot) [_____] repair the damage.

4   I (could not) ☐ believe how much the service cost.

5   The garage (would not) ☐ refund the bill.

6   Why (do not) ☐ you spend more time with customers?

Note: People often confuse 'you're' and 'your'. 'You're' is short for 'you are', while 'your' means belonging to you. Similarly, 'they're' is short for 'they are', while 'there' is a place. If you are not sure, write it in full.

The possessive apostrophe

A lot of people are confused by the possessive apostrophe. Some people try to overcome the problem by putting an apostrophe after any 's' at the end of a word!

It is called the possessive apostrophe because it is used when writing about something that belongs to, or is owned by, a person, place or thing.

An apostrophe followed by 's' ('s) is added to singular words (i.e. where there is only one person, place or thing)

- For example: the mechanic's toolbox = the toolbox belonging to the mechanic (just one mechanic).

D Put the apostrophe in the correct place below.

Her friends car. (one friend)

If the word is plural and already ends with an 's', then you just add an apostrophe at the end of the word (i.e. after the 's')

- For example: her friends' cars = the cars belonging to her friends (more than one friend).

E Put the apostrophe in the correct place below.

The engineers staff room. (More than one engineer)

An apostrophe, followed by 's' ('s) is added to plural words that do not end with an 's'

- For example: the children's toys = the toys belonging to the children.

F Put the apostrophe in the correct place below.

The mens equipment.

How your memory works

The brain

Your brain is like an amazing automotive computer that stores memories and information. There are two types of memory.

Short-term memory holds a small amount of information for a short period of time. It makes particular use of the part of your brain called the 'pre-frontal lobe'.

Long-term memory stores an unlimited amount of information indefinitely.

Facts

- Brains never become full, but they do forget if you do not exercise them.
- Your memory is more likely to remember things that are important or that form a pattern.
- Different parts of the same memory are stored in different parts of your brain.
- Most human beings find handwriting, speech and faces easy to remember.

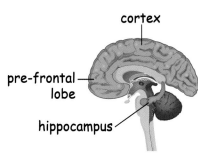

Information is transferred from short-term to long-term memory through a special part of the brain. This part of the brain, called the 'hippocampus', is like a sorting centre where new sensations are compared with previous ones.

When we remember new facts by repeating them or using other memory techniques we are actually passing them through the hippocampus several times. This keeps strengthening the associations among these new elements until the brain has learned to associate these things to create what we call a memory.

The hippocampus is important in what is called **episodic memory**. This lets you remember something years later, like a happy holiday. It allows you to 'play the scene back' by restarting the pattern of the activity in the various parts of the brain.

How to improve your memory

Here are some tips on how to improve your memory:

- **Repetition:** this is the best way to remember things for a short period of time, such as a phone number or ingredients for a recipe.
- **Make up a story:** if you have to remember a list of things, create a story that includes them all. This will make connections between them and you will remember them better.
- **Mental exercise:** games, puzzles and mental arithmetic are like 'brain aerobics'.
- **Physical exercise:** this increases your heart rate and sends more oxygen to your brain, which makes your memory work better.
- **Listen to music:** research shows that listening to relaxing instrumental music helps you to organise ideas more clearly and remember things better.
- **Eat the right things:** food containing omega-3, such as fish, spinach and olive oil, helps to improve your memory. Vitamins C and E (in oranges, strawberries and red grapes) and vitamin B (in meat and green vegetables) are also good for your brain.
- **Control stress:** relaxing, getting enough sleep and positive thinking also help your memory.

A Read the text and answer these questions.

1 What type of memory stores information for a short period?

2 Which part of the brain compares previous sensations with new ones?

3 Name one type of thing that human beings find easy to remember.

4 What is the best way to remember things for a short time?

5 What sends more oxygen to the brain and makes your memory work better?

6 Name a food that contains omega-3.

B What do you remember or forget?

1 Make a note of what you need to remember:

a) at home.

b) at college.

c) at work.

2 What do you do to help you remember?

3 What do you tend to forget?

Share your list with a partner.

C Spend 30 seconds looking at the list of 20 words on page 27 and try to remember as many as you can.

Now write all of the words that you remember here.

- If you remembered at least five, that is good.
- What methods did you use to remember them?
- Did you try making up a story to connect the words?

D Look at the words you wrote down. Did you spell them all correctly?

Jot down here any that you got wrong and try to learn them. Then have another go.

E Write a story to help you remember these words.

work   sandwich   hat   empty   pink   inside   shirt   angry   umbrella   fly

F I went on holiday.

This is a group game for 4 to 10 players.

The first person says, 'I went on holiday and I took …'

They follow this by saying something they might take on holiday, for example, sunglasses.

The second person says, 'I went on holiday and I took sunglasses and …', adding another item, such as a beach towel.

Each person has to remember all of the things that have been said before and add a new one at the end.

If someone forgets an item then they have to drop out.

Play goes on until only one person is left.

Words to remember for Activity C:

fish	blue	five	hand	bucket
sad	today	tall	dress	why
banana	eat	boat	tree	silly
fiddlesticks	wall	star	chair	sleep

SOURCE — Lewis Hamilton – a true champion?

The ups and downs of Lewis Hamilton's career

Lewis Hamilton is one of the most fascinating racing drivers of his generation. His aggressive driving style has won him many fans and his celebrity lifestyle also keeps him in the gossip columns.

He was born in Stevenage in 1985 and began karting at the age of eight. When he was 10 years old, Lewis approached McLaren boss Ron Dennis and asked for his autograph saying, 'Hi. I'm Lewis Hamilton. One day I want to be racing your cars.' Hamilton was very successful in karting, becoming a national champion.

In 1998, when Lewis was aged just 13, the McLaren team gave him a driver development contract. They supported him through the lower categories such as Formula Renault, Formula Three and GP2. In 2007 he joined the Vodafone McLaren Mercedes Formula 1 team as teammate to Fernando Alonso. Alonso was a double world champion and had joined the team from Renault that year. This made Lewis the first black driver to race in a Grand Prix. His first season was little short of sensational. He was frequently quicker than Alonso, taking his first victory at the Canadian Grand Prix in June. Going into the final race at Brazil, he lead the World Championship. However, this race was won by Kimi Räikkönen for Ferrari, who took the championship by one point from Lewis and Alonso.

Lewis quickly became a hero to many F1 fans – partly because of his spectacular driving style and his amazing ability to overtake his rivals on the road. In 2008, his second season in F1, Lewis beat Ferrari's Felipe Massa by one point at the finale in Brazil. This made him not just the first black world champion but also, at just 23 years old, the youngest there had ever been.

Since then Lewis's progress has been less rapid. Major changes to the technical regulations in 2009 made his McLaren less competitive and he came fifth in the championship, which was won by Jenson Button in a Mercedes-powered Brawn.

In the next season, 2010, Button joined Hamilton at McLaren. It was widely expected that Hamilton would prove much faster on the track, but Button's often smoother approach to driving gave him two victories early in the season. Hamilton did not win a Grand Prix until the Turkish round at the end of May but did end up in fourth position overall, with Button fifth. The Red Bull was the car to beat that season, however, with German Sebastian Vettel winning the championship.

Vettel triumphed again in 2011, proving almost unbeatable at times. This year Button finished second in the World Championship while Hamilton finished fifth. One reason for this was that Button's driving style was better suited to the new Pirelli tyres than the style of the more flamboyant Hamilton. Criticisms were also made in the press about Hamilton's celebrity lifestyle away from the track, including his on-off relationship with ex-Pussycat Doll Nicole Scherzinger.

By the end of the 2011 season, F1 enthusiasts were waiting to see what would happen next for Lewis Hamilton.

A Read the text and answer these questions.

1 Who was Lewis Hamilton's first teammate at McLaren?

2 Who sponsored McLaren in 2007?

3 In what year did Hamilton win the World Championship?

4 Where was Lewis Hamilton born?

5 What did Lewis Hamilton drive competitively before he drove cars?

6 Which two things made Lewis Hamilton unique when he won the World Championship?

a)

b)

7 What happened in 2009 that affected his car?

8 What has the press criticised Lewis Hamilton for?

9 Which team did Alonso drive for before he joined McLaren?

10 Where did Lewis Hamilton win his first Grand Prix race?

B Match each driver to the team they have driven for.

Driver		Team
1 Felipe Massa		a) McLaren
2 Jenson Button		b) Ferrari
3 Sebastian Vettel		c) Brawn
4 Lewis Hamilton		d) Red Bull

C Prepare for a discussion about the sponsorship of F1 racing.
Consider the following questions, noting down your answers and the reasons for them.

- Why do companies sponsor F1 racing?

- Before there was company sponsorship, cars raced under their national colours. Do you think that was better?

- Does it matter that Red Bull do not actually make cars?

D Read through the events in Lewis Hamilton's career below and then match each one to the correct date.

Wins the World Championship   Gets first contract with McLaren

Comes fifth in the World Championship   Joins McLaren F1 team

Born in Stevenage   Wins the Turkish Grand Prix

1985:

1998:

2007:

2008:

2010:

2011:

E Insert the correct word in each gap.

Championship   celebrity   black   suited   karting

1 Hamilton became the national [   ] champion.

2 Red Bull won the World [   ] in 2010.

3 Button's smoother driving style was better [   ] to the new Pirelli tyres.

4 Hamilton was the first [   ] driver to compete in a Grand Prix.

5 Hamilton leads a [   ] lifestyle.

F Which of these statements is fact and which is opinion?

1 Lewis Hamilton has a spectacular driving style.   Fact ◯   Opinion ◯

2 Vettel proved almost unbeatable at times.   Fact ◯   Opinion ◯

3 Alonso was a double world champion.   Fact ◯   Opinion ◯

4 Lewis Hamilton features in the gossip columns.   Fact ◯   Opinion ◯

5 Button has a smoother driving style than Hamilton.   Fact ◯   Opinion ◯

G Tobacco companies are no longer allowed to sponsor F1 teams.

Decide whether this is a good thing or a bad thing.

Write a paragraph to support your view that will persuade others to agree with you.

FOCUS ON Non-verbal communication

Non-verbal communication (NVC) is any type of behaviour that is not speech. It is a very powerful communication tool. We are often unaware of the NVC we use.

NVC can be as important as what we say when we are speaking or listening to another person. The NVC used by staff in motor vehicle work is important in communicating both with colleagues and with customers.

Being conscious of your own NVC, and being able to interpret that of others, can help you to understand yourself and others better.

Non-verbal communication includes:

- body language
- vocal signals
- personal presentation.

Body language includes a wide range of things such as facial expression, gestures with hands, arms or legs, posture and eye contact.

Vocal signals mean the tone or pitch of your voice when speaking as well as sounds such as 'Mmmm', 'Aha' and 'Er'. These show that you are listening.

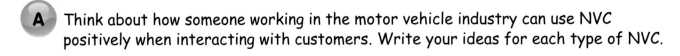

A Think about how someone working in the motor vehicle industry can use NVC positively when interacting with customers. Write your ideas for each type of NVC.

1 Facial expression

2 Gestures

3 Posture

4 Eye contact

5 Tone of voice

B Match each form of NVC to its possible meaning.

NVC
1 Sitting with arms crossed
2 Tight lips
3 Raised eyebrows
4 Slumped in a chair
5 Raised voice
6 Arms by sides, relaxed posture
7 Walking with head up
8 Nodding
9 'Er …'

Possible meaning
a) Agreement
b) Open and welcoming
c) I do not understand
d) Bored, not interested
e) Disagreement
f) Rejection, defensive
g) Disbelief or sarcasm
h) Anger or fear
i) Confident

 C Look at the examples of NVC below. Circle the ones that you think you use frequently.

touching your nose   hands clasped behind head   smiling   tapping fingers

crossing arms   crossing legs   standing up straight   nodding   frowning

avoiding eye contact   making eye contact   hands on hips   tight or pursed lips

Ask a friend if they agree with you.

 **Code of practice for service and repair**

Industry award for Motor Codes

More than 6,800 garages subscribe to the Motor Industry Code of Practice for Service and Repair, which commits them to:

- honest and fair services
- open and transparent pricing
- completing work as agreed
- invoices that match quoted prices
- competent and conscientious staff
- a straightforward, swift complaints procedure.

In November 2011 the code was awarded full Office of Fair Trading (OFT) approval.

And in July 2012 Motor Codes, the industry organisation that operates the code of practice, was recognised for its 'Outstanding Achievement' at the Motor Trader Awards. The accolade recognises the organisation's recent achievements in gaining full OFT approval and the huge boost it has given garages across the country through its motorcodes.co.uk website.

Collecting the award, Motor Codes' Managing Director, Chris Mason, said, 'I am thrilled that the hard work of the Motor Codes team has been recognised at such a prestigious level. We are proud to be leading the charge for better standards of customer service for new car sales, service and repair, while driving business to our nationwide network of subscribers.'

Web traffic on the Motor Codes site has increased dramatically through motorists' use of its Garage Finder tool. Motorists are directed to garage profile pages and from there can choose a service centre that subscribes to the code. There is also an integrated customer survey and garage ranking rewarding those businesses that go above and beyond to be the best.

'With such momentum behind our codes, solid government support and consumer demand for the peace of mind offered by Motor Codes, the message to garages still standing on the sidelines is stop watching and start doing,' continued Mason. 'We have reached a tipping point now where motorists demand high standards and know where to go to get the service they expect: with Motor Codes, quality garages can flourish.'

The Service and Repair Code has grown rapidly since it was set up in 2008, generating custom for subscribed garages that offer a consistent quality of service to motorists. Motor Codes also operates two other codes of practice: for new cars – which now covers 99% of all new car sales – and for vehicle warranty products.

Peace of mind for motorists

A Write down answers to these questions.

1 How many garages subscribe to the code?

2 What is the code of practice called?

3 List two things that customers can expect from a subscribing garage.

a)

b)

B True or false?

1 The Motor Industry Code of Practice for Service and Repair was launched in 2011.　True ◯　False ◯

2 Garages that subscribe to the code commit to completing work as agreed.　True ◯　False ◯

3 Garages that subscribe to the code commit to offering the cheapest prices.　True ◯　False ◯

4 The Motor Codes website has a Garage Finder tool.　True ◯　False ◯

5 Motor Codes operate four codes of practice.　True ◯　False ◯

C Decide whether each of these statements are presented in the text as facts or opinions.

1 In 2008 the motor industry launched the code of practice.　Fact ◯　Opinion ◯

2 We are proud to be leading the charge for better standards of customer service for new car sales, service and repair.　Fact ◯　Opinion ◯

3 In November 2011 the code was awarded full Office of Fair Trading approval.　Fact ◯　Opinion ◯

4 Motorists demand high standards and know where to go to get the service they expect.　Fact ◯　Opinion ◯

D Work with a partner. Add capital letters and full stops to these sentences.

1   in 2008 the motor industry launched a code of practice to improve the standards of garages across the country

2   the office of fair trading has awarded full approval to the code of practice

3   chris mason is the managing director of motor codes

E Read this case study.

Your garage has signed up to the new code of practice. You receive a letter of complaint from a customer about a service the garage carried out recently. Mrs Davidson of 24 Lakes Avenue in your town complains that the service took 30 minutes longer than she had expected, and that the invoice was for £45 more than had been quoted. She also says that she had found that a small amount of oil had leaked from the engine when she went to drive off the next morning.

F Choose the correct answer to the following questions.

1   Why was Mrs Davidson unhappy about the invoice?
   a)   It was £24 more than quoted
   b)   It was £30 more than quoted
   c)   It was £45 more than quoted

2   Which other problem did she complain about?
   a)   The car failed to start the next morning
   b)   There was a small oil leak
   c)   The car had no oil in the engine

G Write a letter replying to the customer. Your letter should include:

- An apology for the problems she has encountered.

- A statement of how you will try to put things right in line with your complaints procedure.

- A clear message that you want to keep her as a valued customer.

(Your address)

(The customer's address)

(Date)

Dear

Yours sincerely

(Your signature)

H In a small group, discuss how a garage you know handles complaints. What should a dissatisfied customer do? Who replies to a complaint? You may like to make notes here.

MOT research reveals worst performers

An analysis of 24.5 m MOT records has revealed that one in five cars registered in 2008 failed its first MOT.

The cars most likely to fail were from French firms Renault, Citroën and Peugeot.

The research, by the consumer website honestjohn.co.uk, involved examining millions of records from the Vehicle Operator and Services Agency (VOSA) through the Government's Open Data scheme. This is data that VOSA has fought to keep secret from car owners for years.

The data shows that between 1 October 2010 and 30 September 2011 one in five cars (352,000 in total) failed their first MOT.

The most common reasons for failure were lighting and signalling, followed closely by tyres, headlight aim and issues with the driver's view of the road.

The worst

European manufacturers are at the bottom of the table for first MOT failures. The worst was Renault. The British-built Mini was second worst, and Citroën was third worst.

Surprisingly, Volvo was one of the 10 worst manufacturers.

This is a shock as its cars traditionally have a reputation for durability. More than 5,800 of the Swedish manufacturer's 26,000 2008-registered cars failed their first MOT.

And the best

The best-performing cars are from Japanese manufacturers, with the top three places going to Lexus, Suzuki and Honda. Saab edges in at number four. The top model was the Suzuki Splash with a 90 per cent pass rate in its first MOT.

Broken down by model, the detailed data reveals that the worst-performing family car was the Renault Megane, with only 71 per cent of cars registered in 2008 passing their first MOT. The Renault Megane was most likely to fail on lighting and signalling

problems, but was also three times more likely to fail on steering faults than the industry average.

The Mini One also performed relatively poorly, with 25 per cent of 2008-registered vehicles failing their first MOT, though this was mainly for minor faults, including lighting and signalling and the driver's view of the road. The publication of these MOT files means that consumers will, for the first time, be able to spot cars' common failures by make, model, year of registration and postcode, based on reliable data.

These MOT files will go a long way to helping the average consumer to make better informed decisions about their next car purchase.

A Read the text and then discuss the following points in your group.

- Was there anything that surprised you in the text?
- In your opinion, which make of car is most reliable?
- Why do you think the top 10 cars are Japanese?
- Why do MOTs matter?

B Choose the correct answer to each question.

1 Which of these is a French firm?

a) Saab ☐

b) Citroën ☐

c) Volvo ☐

2 How many 2008-registered cars failed their first MOT?

a) One in five ☐

b) 25 per cent ☐

c) 26,000 ☐

3 Which manufacturer was the best-performing overall?

a) Suzuki ☐

b) Honda ☐

c) Lexus ☐

4 What is the most common reason for failure?

a) Headlights ☐

b) Lighting and signalling ☐

c) Brakes ☐

5 In which country are the firms of the cars most likely to fail based?

a) Japan ☐

b) Britain ☐

c) France ☐

C Use the text to help you answer these questions.

1 What does VOSA stand for?

_____

2 Why has this data not been available before?

3 Who has made the information available?

D Put these three manufacturers in the right order.

British-built Mini   Citroën   Renault

1 Worst:

2 Second worst:

3 Third worst:

E Choose the correct word to fill the gap in each sentence.

Suzuki   millions   Swedish   purchase   Tyres   minor

1 The website honestjohn.co.uk examined [   ] of records from VOSA.

2 The Mini One failed mainly for [   ] faults.

3 [   ] were the second most common reason for failure.

4 The [   ] Splash had a 90 per cent pass rate in first MOTs.

5 Volvo is a [   ] car manufacturer.

6 The research will help consumers next time they [   ] a car.

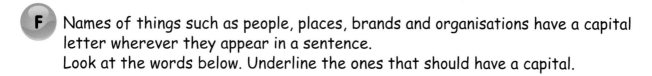
F Names of things such as people, places, brands and organisations have a capital letter wherever they appear in a sentence.
Look at the words below. Underline the ones that should have a capital.

- france
- manufacturer
- renault megane
- british

- postcode
- saab
- european
- millions

G Write a sentence to answer each of these questions.

1   What did the Mini One mainly fail on?

2   Why is it a surprise that Volvo is in the bottom 10?

3   How did honestjohn.co.uk get this information?

H A friend is thinking of buying a three-year-old Renault Megane. Write a note to them saying why they should be careful.

FOCUS ON Commas

There are a number of places where we need to use commas. The main ones are:

- in lists
- to separate parts of sentences
- to replace brackets.

We will look at these in turn.

Commas in a list

We use commas to separate items in a list.

- For example: The store held parts for brakes, exhausts and clutches.

A   Add commas to separate items in these sentences.

1   An exhaust has a manifold a pipe and a silencer.

2   A reliable garage will have honest prices accurate invoices and competent staff.

3   When servicing a gearbox you should check the oil level carry out a visual inspection and do a road test.

4   Dave's lunchbox contained a sandwich a biscuit and a banana.

Separating parts of sentences

We also use a comma to separate two parts of a sentence. Often the comma marks off introductory words.

- For example: In the UK, we drive on the left side of the road.

Sometimes the comma and a linking word, such as 'but' or 'although', join two possible sentences together.

- For example: Bert was 63 and tried to keep up with the latest technology, although he sometimes found it hard.

B   Add commas to separate the two parts of these sentences.

1   In F1 racing too many accidents are caused by reckless driving.

2   To reduce accidents new rules have been established.

3   Following complaints from customers the garage was closed down.

4   Most motor vehicle engineers are male but some women are entering the profession.

Commas instead of brackets

In this case two commas mark off part of a sentence.

- For example: An estate car, also called a station wagon, has a larger internal capacity.

C Add two commas to each of these sentences.

1   Ahmed the Audi specialist will look at your car.

2   Steve Brook from the National Consumer Council thinks that motorists should get a better deal.

3   Seat belts which must be fitted by law minimise the risk of serious injury.

4   Graham Watson the garage owner said it would never happen again.

Getting a feel for commas

If you are not sure about whether to use a comma, try reading the sentence aloud.
If you feel you need to pause, you may need a comma (as in this sentence!).

D Read this passage out loud and decide where to put commas.

Harry has worked on Fords Renaults and Vauxhalls. He prefers Fords as they are

easy and straightforward to service. His current employer Drivesafe is a good

company to work for. Drivesafe treats its staff well giving them generous bonuses

and a good pension scheme.

E Write three sentences here. They can be about anything at all. Then read them out aloud. Do you need to use commas?

1

2

3

MANAGING TIME

Managing time is important both for your work and your studies. It helps you to get the right balance between your work and personal life.

In motor vehicle engineering you need to work quickly and efficiently while making sure you do not miss any faults. You need to plan your work but also be able to deal with unexpected problems. You have to monitor your use of time as it is charged to the customer. And you need to keep on top of records, service plans and other paperwork.

The starting point for managing your time is having clear priorities. What are the things that really matter? It is easy to spend too much time on the urgent things that keep cropping up every day and to lose sight of the more important jobs. So make sure you know what is most important. It can help to talk to your supervisor or tutor about this.

One helpful way of keeping yourself organised is to make a list of the things you need to do in the day. This gives you a clear idea of how much you need to do and how much time you can allow for each task. It is also satisfying when you start ticking off the jobs you have finished.

If you have a big task to do, like an assignment, try breaking it down into smaller tasks. According to the saying, the way to eat an elephant is one bite at a time!

Managing time does not always mean doing things quickly. It is always worth taking the time to do a job well. This can save time in the end as you do not waste time having to do something again because you rushed it first time round.

At the same time, make sure you have breaks during the day. If you have a lunch break and, ideally, get out for some fresh air or exercise, you will come back fresher and with more energy.

A True or false?

Which of these statements are true and which are false, according to the article?

1 It is important to be clear about your priorities.   True ◯   False ◯

2 Unexpected problems help you to manage time.   True ◯   False ◯

3 It is easy to spend too much time on urgent things.   True ◯   False ◯

4 It is a good idea to work through your lunch break.   True ◯   False ◯

5 It is always worth taking the time to do a job well.   True ◯   False ◯

B Write down answers to these questions.

1 Why is time management important?

2 What is the starting point for time management?

3 What is a helpful way of keeping organised?

4 State two ways in which a to-do list can help.

a)

b)

5 What is it good to do in your lunch break?

C In a group, discuss your own time management.

Here are some of the things that make it harder for people to manage their time well.

1 Which are true for you?

2 Which are true for other people you know?

3 Who has good ideas about how to avoid these problems?

Which of these things do you do?	Often	Sometimes	Never
Leave things until the last minute			
Forget to do important things			
Find it hard to say 'No'			
Spend time on things that do not matter			
Spend too much time on the phone			
Spend too much time on Facebook			
Get distracted easily			

D Fill in the gaps in this paragraph using these words:

list   break   important   organised   distracted   priority   smaller

It is important to know which of your tasks are top [   ]. Find time for the things that are [   ] but not urgent. If you keep a to-do [   ], this will help you stay [   ]. Make sure you take a [   ] during the day as this will help you to stay fresh. Avoid getting [   ] by things that are not important. Break up big jobs into [   ] tasks as this can make them more manageable.

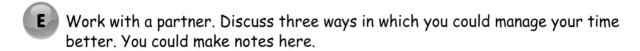

E Work with a partner. Discuss three ways in which you could manage your time better. You could make notes here.

1

2

3

F Write a to-do list below.

1 Make a list here of things you need to do this week.

2 Which are the most important?

Working in teams and with partners

Teamwork and partnership working is very important in motor vehicle sales and repair. This is because a typical garage or workshop brings together a range of people from different occupations and backgrounds.

A definition of a team is:

> **People working together to achieve a common goal or mission. Their work is interdependent and team members share responsibility for achieving the results.**

You will work in a team with your colleagues, as well as other people, who could include sales staff, receptionists, assessors, parts advisers, technicians, mechanics, tyre fitters, welders, supervisors and managers.

The key principles of effective teamwork are:

- having shared or common goals
- openness and honesty
- trust and respect
- reliability and commitment.

Communication

Good communication is essential to the smooth running of teams. It provides the basis for positive interpersonal relationships and ensures that goals and procedures are clear. There are two ways in which team members or partnership workers communicate with each other:

- **Orally**, by speaking and listening. In spoken communication, tone of voice and body language are as important as what we actually say.
- **In writing**, through instructions, notes and emails. Written communication needs to be clear so that the message cannot be misunderstood.

Effective teams

Here are four characteristics of effective teams – and what can happen if they are not in place.

An effective team has:

- a strong sense of purpose and shared goals
- clear roles and responsibilities
- clear procedures that everyone understands
- good relationships between team members.

If this is not in place:

- there will be reduced effort and low energy
- there is less accountability and more conflict
- more time and effort will be needed to achieve tasks
- it will result in tension and stress and there will be less focus on the goals and tasks.

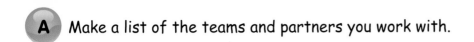

A Make a list of the teams and partners you work with.

Share your list with a partner or the rest of your group.

B Read the text and answer these questions.

1 What can happen if a team does not have clear procedures?

2 Name two things that are important in oral communication.

3 What can cause a team to lack energy and make less effort?

4 Why is good communication important in teamwork?

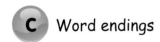

C Word endings

When an ending, or suffix, is added to a word, sometimes the word stays the same and sometimes the final letter 'e' is removed.

- For example:
  - argue, argument, arguing
  - enhance, enhancement, enhancing

Add 'ment' and 'ing' to these words.

Word	+ ment	+ ing
1 achieve		
2 treat		
3 encourage		
4 require		
5 appoint		
6 amaze		

D For each of the following words, write a sentence that contains the word.

1 Reliability

2 Accountable

3 Tension

E Write a short note describing what the team you work in does that makes it effective.

F Read the case study and answer the questions below.

Case study: Organising the import team

Hyundai Car UK's import team is based at Tilbury Docks and handles over 33,000 cars every year. The team carries out a wide range of tasks; it unloads the vehicles, carries out pre-delivery inspections and fits special items such as alarms and music systems. Staff at Tilbury are split over three areas: office, administration and managers; workshop staff; and drivers. Although these three groups of people work together, because their roles were separate there was little understanding or empathy with colleagues' daily issues. The management team at Tilbury wanted to improve collaboration, develop more of a sense of team, and help their staff to get a better understanding of each others' roles and daily pressures.

1 Where is Hyundai Car UK's import team based?

2 What are the three groups of staff?

3 What problem was making it harder for people to work together?

4 Which three changes did the management team want to implement?

a)

b)

c)

FOCUS ON Questions

It may seem obvious what a question is, but people are often not sure when a question mark is needed.

A question is a statement that asks for information. For example:

* Where do you work?
* Which tool should I use for this job?

A Look at the statements below. Put either a question mark or a full stop at the end of each line.

1 What is the cost of the service ⬭

2 The new model comes with air conditioning ⬭

3 When can we start work ⬭

4 When will the car be delivered ⬭

5 The car will be delivered on Tuesday morning ⬭

6 How long will the paint take to dry ⬭

Question words

Some words are used regularly at the start of a question, such as 'why', 'when', 'who', 'how', 'where', 'what'.

B Insert a word at the start of these statements to make a question.

1 [   ] is your favourite food?

2 [   ] is your appointment with the doctor?

3 [   ] do you live?

4 [   ] time do you need to catch the bus?

5 [   ] does she manage to do so much?

Asking questions

In motor vehicle work you will need to ask a lot of questions! You will often have to be careful about how you phrase them.

For example, if a customer brings in a car for a repair quote after an accident, you could just ask: 'What happened?'

But it is more polite to say: 'Can you tell me what happened?'

Wording your question in this way is more polite and sounds more like a request than a demand or instruction.

C Try wording these requests more tactfully.

1 What do you want to drink?

2 Will you put that down? You will break it.

3 Give me the maintenance schedule.

Open and closed questions

There are two types of questions: 'open' and 'closed' ones.

Closed questions often invite 'yes' or 'no' or very brief answers. They do not open up a conversation, but are good for checking details.

- For example: 'Have you checked the delivery?'

An open question needs a longer answer, allowing someone to give you more information or tell you how they think and feel. Open questions often start with 'how', 'what', 'which' and 'why'.

- For example: 'What did the delivery contain?

D 'Rewrite these closed questions as open ones.

1 Did your meeting go well?

2 Do you like working on reception?

3 Have you had a good day?

This does not mean you should not use closed questions. They are useful for finding out precise facts or checking information.

Compare the market

Mazda MX-5

Pros: Great fun to drive, stylish looks, available with metal folding roof, superb value for money.
Cons: Not very practical, no air-con on entry-level models.

The third-generation of the MX-5 is the most sophisticated yet. The classic charm of the original has been brought up to date. It's now a much easier convertible to live with on an everyday basis. It has a comfortable ride, modern and functional interior and less wind noise in the cabin.

Ford Focus

Pros: Excellent ride and versatile handling, spacious, strong 1.6 litre EcoBoost petrol and 2.0 litre diesel engines.

Cons: Electronic steering gives little feedback, confusing Powershift gear change, seats need more lateral support.

The Ford Focus is the perfect all-round car especially for a young family. It's nice to drive, practical, cheap to run as well as affordable. It's also well equipped with safety features, so it is no surprise it is a popular seller.

BMW X1

Pros: Economical diesel engines with low CO_2 emissions, available with two- or four-wheel drive, large boot area.
Cons: Some rather cheap-feeling interior plastics, firm ride.

This is BMW's fourth X model and is also the smallest. However, it has much of the practicality and spaciousness of its larger counterparts. It's slightly shorter than a 3-series which makes it easy to manoeuvre and park, especially in town, but still has impressive space for passengers in the back as well as a large and useful boot.

Audi Q3

Pros: Affordable entry to Q models, available with two- or four-wheel drive, stylish looks.
Cons: Fails to match rivals for driver engagement, options can make it pricey, interior space is a little tight.

With the success of the Audi Q7 and Q5 models, it was almost inevitable that Audi would introduce a smaller entry-level to the Q range. It's a much better-looking model compared to its closest competitor and the prestige that comes with the name should mean that this smallest Q model will be a sales success.

A Write the make of car next to each description.

Description	Name of car
1 Economical diesel engine	
2 No air-con on entry models	
3 Versatile handling	
4 Options make it pricey	
5 Cheap interior plastics	
6 Fun to drive	
7 Confusing gear change	
8 Two- or four-wheel drive	

B Read the text and answer these questions.

1 Which car has a large boot?

2 Which two cars look stylish?

a)

b)

3 Which car is a convertible?

4 Which car is spacious and practical?

5 Give two reasons why the Ford Focus is a good choice for a young family?

6 Give two reasons why the Audi Q3 will be a sales success.

C Which car do you think is the best choice?

Make notes of the reasons for your choice in preparation for a group discussion. You can include other things you know about the car or the make in your points.

D Choose a word from the list below to fill the gap in each sentence.

folding   wind   interior   manoeuvre   support

1   The seats in the Ford Focus do not give enough [   ].

2   The Mazda MX-5 has a [   ] roof.

3   The BMW X1 is easy to [   ] and park.

4   The [   ] space in the Audi Q3 is a bit tight.

5   The level of [   ] noise in the Mazda MX-5 has been reduced.

E Read the text below and then answer the questions.

CO_2 emissions

Cars make a significant contribution to overall emissions of CO_2 in the UK. In urban areas, road transport is also one of the major sources of emissions that are harmful to human health.

Climate change, often referred to as global warming, is thought to be one of the greatest environmental threats facing the world today. When petrol, diesel or some other fuels are burnt for energy in an engine, the main by-products are water and carbon dioxide (CO_2) and nitrogen (N_2). Although not directly harmful to human health, CO_2 is the main greenhouse gas contributing to climate change.

1   Which car in the reviews has low CO_2 emissions?

2   What is another term for climate change?

F   True or false?

Which of these statements are true and which are false?

1   CO_2 is directly harmful to human health.   True ◯   False ◯

2   Water is produced when a car burns petrol.   True ◯   False ◯

3   Cars give out emissions that are harmful to human health.   True ◯   False ◯

4   CO_2 contributes to climate change.   True ◯   False ◯

G   'Pro' means for, or on behalf of, and 'con' comes from contra, which means against.
Therefore, pros and cons are arguments for and against something.
Make a list of the pros and cons of a car that you are familiar with.

Hybrid cars becoming more mainstream

The days when hybrid cars could be dismissed as a passing technical novelty are well and truly past: figures from the Society of Motor Manufacturers and Traders (SMMT) show a steady rise in annual UK sales over the past five years.

From 2007 up to the end of March 2012, almost 100,000 hybrid vehicles were sold in the UK, helping achieve a healthy saving in carbon emissions. In terms of UK market share, hybrid cars have gone from 0.7 per cent to 1.3 per cent over the same period.

Toyota and Lexus alone sold over 77,000 hybrid cars in the UK in the five years to 2012, largely due to the success of the Prius.

Most hybrid cars that are available in the UK have CO_2 emissions that drop below the 100 g/km mark, qualifying them for congestion charge exemption in London and free VED road tax. With lower CO_2 fuel economy is increased, which may help explain the growing sales at a time of continuously rising fuel prices.

2012 should see further impetus for even more drivers to make the switch, with four new hybrids being introduced by Toyota and Lexus. Toyota has downsized its hybrid technology so that it can fit into more of their models, with the introduction of the Yaris Hybrid in the summer of 2012, promising a class-best combination of emissions and efficiency without reducing the amount of space on board or in the boot.

At the other end of the size scale, the summer will also mark the debut of Prius+ MPV, the first seven-seat full hybrid in Europe. The new range will deliver CO_2 emissions below 100 g/km, earning VED road tax and London congestion charge exemption.

Several manufacturers, in particular Peugeot and Citroën, have been working on the world's first diesel hybrid cars, with the recent launch of Peugeot's 3008 and Citroën's DS5, both of which share the same HYbrid4 drivetrain technology.

Plug-in hybrids are also beginning to enter the market, with the launch of the Prius plug-in hybrid coming soon, giving increased efficiency compared to the existing Toyota Prius. The arrival of two range-extended electric vehicle models is also imminent, which are essentially hybrids with both an electric motor and conventional engine used for propulsion. The Vauxhall Ampera and Chevrolet Volt have already gathered significant interest and won several awards.

Jon Williams, Toyota President and Managing Director said: 'The SMMT data show how the momentum for hybrid is increasing. Motorists appreciate its environmental performance, its reliability and ease of use, plus the smooth and refined driving quality.

'Toyota's leadership in hybrid technology offers a proven, flexible technology with which we will be able to develop and deliver sustainable transport with minimum environmental impact.'

A steady rise in annual UK sales over the past five years

A Read the text and answer this question.
What are the two main purposes of the text 'Hybrid cars becoming more mainstream'?

1

2

B According to the text, what share of the UK car market did hybrid cars have by March 2012?

1 0.7 per cent ⃝

2 1.3 per cent ⃝

3 1.7 per cent ⃝

4 13 per cent ⃝

C According to the text, which one of these statements is true?

1 The Peugeot 3008 was planned for summer 2012. ⃝

2 The Vauxhall Ampera was planned for summer 2012. ⃝

3 The Toyota Yaris hybrid was planned for summer 2012. ⃝

4 The Citroën DS5 was planned for summer 2012. ⃝

D According to the text, give two reasons why there has been an increase in the sales of hybrid cars between 2007 and 2012.

1

2

E Which of these statements are presented in the text as fact and which as opinion?

1 Between 2007 and March 2012, almost
   100,000 hybrid vehicles were sold in the UK.   Fact ◯   Opinion ◯

2 Toyota and Lexus sold over 77,000 hybrid
   cars in the UK in the five years to 2012.   Fact ◯   Opinion ◯

3 Peugeot and Citroën have been working on
   diesel hybrid cars.   Fact ◯   Opinion ◯

4 Motorists appreciate the smooth and
   refined driving quality of hybrid cars.   Fact ◯   Opinion ◯

5 Toyota will be able to deliver sustainable
   transport with minimum environmental impact.   Fact ◯   Opinion ◯

F The text claims that 'The days when hybrid cars could be dismissed as a passing technical novelty are well and truly past'.
From your reading of the text, give two examples to show how this text might be biased.

1

2

G Read the text again and identify the main points that it contains.
You can do this in several ways. For example, you can:

- use a highlighter pen or underline key phrases or sentences

- cross out sentences (or paragraphs) that you will not need

- make notes here of the key words and phrases.

H Draft a 150-word summary of the text for someone interested in buying a hybrid car.
The original article is around 450 words long and your task is to cut it down to about 150 words.

- In the space below or on a separate piece of paper, make notes of the main points.

- Read the article again to check that you have included all of the main points.

- Write up your summary, using your notes rather than the original article – this will help you to use your own words where possible.

I Check what you have written.

- Is the length right (around 150 words)?

- Have you included all of your main points?

- Is the summary clear and concise?

- Is the punctuation and spelling OK?

Make any changes that you want to make.

FOCUS ON Audience and purpose

Whenever you say or write anything, you need to be clear about:

* who you are speaking or writing to – your **audience**
* why you are speaking or writing – your **purpose**.

This is especially important when you are planning a letter, report, talk or presentation.

Your audience

Things to think about for your audience include:

* who they are and whether you know them already
* why they will read or listen to what you write or say
* what is likely to interest them
* which style is likely to be appropriate and inappropriate
* how much they know about the subject
* whether they will know technical terms
* whether they may have any difficulty listening or reading.

A Who might be the audience for each of these items?

Possible audiences: tutor, manager, fellow students, work colleagues, friends.

1 Assignment for your course

2 Text saying where to meet tonight

3 Talk about a work placement

4 Report about a vehicle recall

B If you are writing an assignment for your tutor, which of these statements are true and which are false?

1 You should use a formal style.   True ◯   False ◯

2 You should make it amusing.   True ◯   False ◯

3 You should have a clear structure.   True ◯   False ◯

4 You should not include technical terms.   True ◯   False ◯

5 You should stick to the topic.   True ◯   False ◯

Your purpose

Common purposes for speaking and writing include:

- to inform
- to explain
- to impress
- to persuade
- to entertain.

When you plan a talk or piece of writing, make sure you are clear about your purpose and what you want people to know, understand and do as a result of what they hear or read.

C Read the following text.

The rigid axle arrangement is one of the simplest constructions to connect left- and right-hand wheels together and allow them to move with the suspension system. Because it is so simple, it is still used by manufacturers today. Key advantages include:

- a low number of components
- requires little service maintenance
- wheels alter their alignment as the axle moves, providing low tyre wear.

Who is the audience, and what is the purpose of this text?

D Read the following text.

The motor industry operates a code of practice called Motor Codes that is designed to improve the standards of garages across the country. The Managing Director of Motor Codes said, 'With such momentum behinds our codes, solid government support and consumer demand for the peace of mind offered by Motor Codes, the message to garages still standing on the sidelines is stop watching and start doing.'

Who is the audience, and what is the purpose of this text?

 **Communicating with colleagues**

GIVE AND TAKE

Anyone who works with the public needs good communication skills. You must be able to communicate well with customers, but it is also vital to communicate well with your colleagues – the other people you work with.

An important part of being a good communicator is being sensitive to other people. This can involve three key things:

- Respect – which means showing other people that you care about them or value their views by behaving in a respectful way.
- Empathy – which means trying to understand another person's feelings as if they were your own – 'putting yourself in their shoes'.
- Trust – which means showing other people that they can count on you to do what you say you will do, and to support them.

Good communication with colleagues also depends on good information sharing.

- Giving information – you may need to pass on information about a job to a workmate, you may need to report something to your manager, or you may need to give a customer some details about their car. In all of these cases you need to remember to share the information promptly, clearly and accurately.
- Listening carefully to what other people say – you will also receive information from colleagues. You need to listen to what they say, and check if you have not understood something properly.

Bear in mind that several things can get in the way of sharing information as well. Barriers to communication can result from:

- the way the message is communicated – for example, using ambiguous words or phrases, using complex technical terms, mumbling, or writing badly
- the way the message is received – for example, the person listening or reading may be tired, hard of hearing or may not understand the language used
- the environment – for example, a noisy area, interruptions from other people, an email not getting through or a crackly mobile phone line.

Good communication also depends on being prepared to ask for help, advice and support when you need it, and being prepared to accept offers of help from colleagues. In turn, you should be prepared and ready to offer help, advice and support when this is appropriate.

A Match these terms to their definitions.

Terms	Definitions
1 Respect	a) showing other people that they can count on you
2 Empathy	b) showing other people that you care about them or value their views
3 Trust	c) trying to understand another person's feelings as if they were your own

B Write down answers to these questions.

1 Which two groups of people must a motor vehicle technician communicate with?

2 From the text, choose three examples of when you need to give information.

3 Write down the three barriers to communication that are mentioned in the text.

 **C** In your group read this text.

People may not contribute fully to a discussion because they are shy or lack confidence; they may feel they do not know enough about a topic to contribute; or they may be put off because other people dominate the discussion. You can find ways of encouraging them to say things without them feeling threatened.

In your group, discuss:

- things you can do before a discussion to help people participate
- things you can do during the discussion to help everyone feel involved
- things that might discourage people from participating that you should avoid during discussions.

D Reflect on how well the discussion went.
Look at these pairs of statements and decide in each case whether statement A or statement B was more true of your group discussion.

Statement A					Statement B
The discussion had a clear focus.	4	3	2	1	The purpose of the discussion was vague.
Everybody participated.	4	3	2	1	One or two people talked most of the time.
The discussion was lively and interesting.	4	3	2	1	The discussion was dull and boring.
The discussion stayed focused on the point.	4	3	2	1	The discussion often wandered off the point.
The discussion moved on from one topic to the next.	4	3	2	1	The discussion got bogged down in one topic.
We covered all of the discussion points.	4	3	2	1	We only covered one or two discussion points.
We ended on time.	4	3	2	1	We went well over time.

 E Read this text with a partner.

Ground rules

Formal discussions need certain rules if they are to work well. Ground rules set out the behaviours that are or are not acceptable in the group. They can include:

- practical rules (e.g. we arrive on time)
- rules about how we work (e.g. we only have one conversation at a time)
- rules about how we interact (e.g. we listen to what each other says).

Ground rules help a group to operate effectively and to create a positive and constructive atmosphere. If everyone takes part in agreeing the ground rules, they are more likely to follow them than if one person imposes them.

Identify two ways in which you could have helped the discussion to go better.

1

2

F Use this checklist to help you move discussions forward.

Discussions can get bogged down, and you can find yourself spending too much time on one issue and then having to rush through other important topics. Here are some techniques for helping to move a discussion forward.

- ☐ Give a short summary of what has been said.
- ☐ Remind the group about the time that is available.
- ☐ If contributions are not relevant, gently remind people of the topic.
- ☐ If two or three people are dominating the discussion, invite other people to contribute who have not yet done so.
- ☐ If you get bogged down on a topic, consider asking one or two people to take this forward after the meeting.
- ☐ Try to draw a topic to an end by saying, for example, 'It sounds as if we have agreed that …'.
- ☐ Encourage the group to move on by saying, for example, 'Should we move on to the next topic now?'

 G Write a message.

At times you may need to leave a written message for a colleague or your manager.

You have been working on a Renault Clio. The customer reported erratic steering but you have not been able to pinpoint the source of the problem. You did a test drive and found that the car was veering to the right. You have contacted the customer to tell them that their car will not be ready today. However, you will not be in tomorrow as you are on a training course. Write a message explaining the situation to the person who will need to take over the job.

Write your message here.

SOURCE Car or computer network?

On-board computer systems

Many trainers working in the motor industry comment on how a modern car technician needs a different skill set from their predecessors of a generation ago. Whereas the mechanic who trained on cars from the 1960s needed to know about purely mechanical things like brake linings, today's apprentices need to have significant understanding of computer software. This came to a head recently when Toyota recalled their Prius models because of a software glitch.

What do computers in cars do?

All cars manufactured today contain several computers. They are in charge of monitoring engine emissions and adjusting the engine to keep emissions as low as possible. The computers receive information from many different sensors, including:

- the oxygen sensor
- the air flow metre
- the air temperature sensor
- the engine temperature sensor
- the throttle position sensor
- the knock sensor.

Using the information from these sensors, the computer can control things such as the fuel injectors, spark plugs and the idle speed to get the best performance possible from the engine while keeping emissions low. The computer can also sense when something has gone wrong and can inform the driver with the 'check engine' light. A technician can read a diagnostic code from the computer and fix the problem.

What computers can you expect to find?

Depending on how expensive the car is, different on-board computers may be included, for example:

- a computer that controls the automatic **transmission**
- a car with anti-lock **brakes** has a computer reading the wheel speed and controlling the brakes
- **airbag** systems have their own computers
- a car with keyless entry or a **security** system has a computer for these systems
- advanced **climate control** systems often have computers
- some cars now have computers that can remember the settings for multiple drivers for **motorised seats and mirrors**
- any **radio** or **CD player** with a digital display contains a computer of its own
- **cruise control** systems use computers.

In other words, a modern luxury car is a rolling computer network. It is amazing how many embedded controllers a car can have.

A What is the main purpose of the text 'On-board computer systems'?

B True or false?

Which of these statements are true and which are false, according to the text?

1 A mechanic who trained on cars from the 1960s needed to know about computer systems.　　True ◯　　False ◯

2 Toyota recalled its Prius models because of a mechanical fault.　　True ◯　　False ◯

3 The computer can inform the driver of a fault with the 'check engine' light.　　True ◯　　False ◯

4 In some cars a computer can remember the mirror setting for each individual driver.　　True ◯　　False ◯

C Give three features of the text that help to convey information.

1 [　　　　　　　　　　　　　　　　　　　　　　　　　　　]

3 [　　　　　　　　　　　　　　　　　　　　　　　　　　　]

3 [　　　　　　　　　　　　　　　　　　　　　　　　　　　]

D The text states that 'All cars manufactured today contain at least one computer'. Give two examples from the text of what this computer may do.

1

2

E Your friend is interested in buying a car. From your reading of the text, what three types of computer controls would you suggest they consider?

1

2

3

F Choose a word from the list below to fill the gap in each sentence.

consumption   functions   store   distance   on-board   travelled

A trip computer is an [   ] computer found in many of today's cars. It has

various [   ] such as recording distance [   ], current fuel

consumption, average fuel [   ], average speed and the [   ]

you may be able to travel before you next need to fill up the petrol tank. Some trip

computers measure this information for one trip; others can [   ]

information for several trips.

G In a group, discuss examples of car computer systems.

- Which car computer systems have you come across?
- What do they do?
- What are their benefits?
- Do they have disadvantages?

H You receive this email from a friend of your father.

From: Mike (mike@email.com)
To: You (you@email.com)
Subject: Car computers

Hi

We need to replace our car before it breaks down completely and we plan to get a new or nearly new model. But I am confused about some of the jargon the saleswoman used.

The car seems to be full of computers. What is a trip computer? Is it the same as a sat nav? Will it be difficult to use?

She also said something about a computer-aided radio and CD player, and apparently it has motorised mirrors with multiple driver settings.

You know more about these things than I do. Are they a good idea? Or should we be looking for something older and simpler?

Mike

Write an email reply. Answer Mike's questions based on the text and your own knowledge.

From: You (you@email.com)
To: Mike (mike@email.com)
Subject: Re: Car computers

FOCUS ON Checking written work

Checking what you have written is really important. It is not just people who struggle with spelling who need to check their work. We all make mistakes without meaning to, especially when using a word processor.

Think about publishers – they employ proofreaders to check books before they are printed even though they have been written by professional writers.

A Read these tips about how to proofread your work. There are some mistakes, or 'typos'. Underline the ones you find.

Proofreading tips

Profreading is the task of reading and correcting wirtten work. Its best to proofread a paper copy, rather than checking on screen as you will spot erors more easily.

You need to concentrate to do proof reading. Find a quite space where you will not distracted. First, scan your document to make sure the layout is clear Mark anything that looks odd and check pargraphs and headings.

When checking n detail you might put a ruler or peice of paper below the line you are reading to help you focus? Each sentence should start with a capital leter and end with appropriate punctutation such as a fullstop or question mark:

All words must be spelt correct. You can use a dictionery or spellchecker, but you need to be careful with spell checkers as they wont always pick up the right word for the meaning. They will miss spellinh mistakes when a typing error has changed one word ibnto another perfectly good one, such as learner/leaner, where/were, to/too.

B Write the correct spelling of any words that were misspelt.

Which documents need to be checked?

You should check everything you write. Just one missing word in an email to a friend can completely change the meaning or cause confusion, for example if you are making an arrangement to meet. But not everything needs to be perfect.

C Tick the documents below that you think need to be thoroughly checked.

- ☐ A note to your mum saying you have gone out and when you will be back
- ☐ An email applying for a job
- ☐ An assignment for your course
- ☐ An email to a friend

Proofreading checklist

Use this checklist when you proofread an important document.

- ☐ Scan the whole document – is the layout neat and clear?
- ☐ Look at the paragraphs – they do not all have to be the same length, but are there any that are very long or very short?
- ☐ Are your headings clear with consistent use of fonts and spacing?
- ☐ Is the order logical and do the headings help to sequence the content?
- ☐ Check the titles, captions and position of any tables or illustrations.
- ☐ Read every sentence and word to look for errors.
- ☐ Make sure every sentence makes sense and conveys a complete idea.
- ☐ If you make a correction, read through the whole sentence again to check that it makes sense.
- ☐ Check sentence punctuation. Do all sentences begin with a capital letter and end with a full stop, question mark or exclamation mark?
- ☐ Check you have spelt any proper names correctly and used capital letters where they are needed.
- ☐ If you have used quotations in inverted commas, make sure you have used either single (') or double (") inverted commas consistently.
- ☐ Check that references at the end of the document are complete and use the required form.

Ask a friend

It is a good idea to ask someone else to proofread your work. This is because when we check our own work we see what we meant to write rather than what we have actually written. Someone else may spot errors that we miss.

And checking someone else's work will help you to recognise problems and avoid them yourself in the future.

SOURCE **A good impression**

SUCCEEDING IN INTERVIEWS

You should see any sort of job interview as a two-way exchange of information. The interviewer is trying to find out some important things about you – your skills, attitudes, experience and interests – to help them decide whether you are the right person for the job. At the same time you want to find out more about the organisation or company so that you can work out if this is the right job for you.

FIRST IMPRESSIONS REALLY COUNT

It is a sad fact that people form an opinion of someone in the first 10 seconds or so of meeting them. In an interview that can make a big difference to your chances of getting the job. It can be very difficult to recover from a bad first impression. Below is a breakdown of the importance of three key factors in making a good impression, based on research.

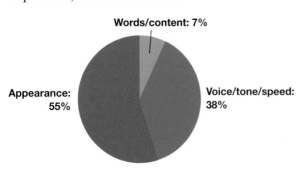

Words/content: 7%

Appearance: 55%

Voice/tone/speed: 38%

In other words, the *way* that you look and the *way* that you talk are more important than *what* you say.

One aspect of appearance is your body language – how you walk and stand, gestures and facial expression. Even the interviewer may not be aware that they are responding to this.

USE BODY LANGUAGE WELL

- Smile at the beginning of the interview and look at the interviewer.
- Offer a firm handshake.
- Sit back into your seat. This can help you to look and feel more confident.
- Do not cross your arms – folded arms can make you appear unfriendly and defensive and can be a barrier to communication.
- Maintain regular eye contact with the interviewer but do not stare at them.
- Respond to the interviewer with gestures such as nods and turn towards them to show that you are listening.

THE WAY THAT YOU LOOK

If you search the internet for tips on how to dress for an interview you will find that quite a few sites recommend formal dress – smart suit/dress, tie, etc. But in some sectors, formal clothes may not be appropriate, so the best advice is to choose the most *suitable* clothing. Here are a few tips in terms of appearance:

- Wear clothes in which you feel comfortable and confident.
- Make sure that your clothes are clean and tidy, including your shoes.
- Make sure that you have a bath or shower on the morning of your interview.
- Make sure that you look well groomed. This means neat hair, clean nails, face and so on.
- Do not wear revealing clothes, anything too wacky, too much make-up or jewellery.
- Do not smoke just before an interview – if you feel you must smoke, use a breath freshener.

A Read the text and choose the correct answer.

1 What is the most important factor in making a good impression?

   a) Your tone of voice ⬭

   b) What you say ⬭

   c) Your appearance ⬭

2 Which of the following is a form of body language?

   a) Smiling ⬭

   b) Wearing revealing clothes ⬭

   c) Smoking ⬭

3 How long does it usually take someone to form an opinion of you?

   a) Approximately a minute ⬭

   b) About 10 seconds ⬭

   c) Five minutes ⬭

4 How should you dress for an interview?

   a) You should always wear a jacket or suit ⬭

   b) You should choose suitable clothing ⬭

   c) You should wear clothes that will grab the interviewer's attention ⬭

5 What advice is given about eye contact?

   a) Look the interviewer in the eyes as often as possible ⬭

   b) Do not look the interviewer in the eyes – it is bad manners ⬭

   c) Make regular eye contact but do not stare ⬭

B Think about the main 'selling points' that you can offer a potential employer.

- What jobs or work experience have you had?
- What skills and qualifications do you have?
- What tools and equipment can you use?
- What aspects of your personality or attitudes make you a good employee?

C Think of a job that you would like to do.

If you got a job interview tomorrow, what would you wear?

Share your answer with a partner.

D Write a short description of a job that you would like to do. It should include:

- the job title
- the organisation or company
- what the job involves
- what skills they are looking for
- what sort of person they are looking for.

E Using the job description you have written, think about how you would answer the following questions in an interview for a job or a work experience placement.

1 What interests you about this job or place of work?

2 How would this job/placement help you with your course or future career?

3 Why are you suitable for this job/placement?

F What you say in an interview matters, but listening effectively can be just as important.

1 Why do you think that listening in an interview is important?

2 How can you use body language to show that you are listening?

G Work in groups of three. Decide on a job that you could all do, or choose one of the job descriptions from exercise D.
Take it in turns to interview each other for the job, with one person acting as interviewer, one as interviewee and one observing. The observer will complete the checklist below.
Start the interview by walking into the room and sitting down. The interviews only need to be about five minutes long.

First impressions				Manners
	✓		✓	
Excellent		5		Charming
Good		4		Agreeable
Satisfactory		3		Satisfactory
Not very good		2		Awkward
Unfavourable		1		Offensive
Oral communication				**Body language**
	✓		✓	
Excellent choice of words		5		Very effective
Good choice of words		4		Good, positive
Sometimes lost for words		3		Limited, neutral
Limited vocabulary		2		Poor, would not impress
Poor		1		Would create a negative effect

Tips for talking
- As with appearance, the important thing is to come across as comfortable and natural.
- Use correct grammar.
- Speak clearly.
- Do not talk too loudly or too quietly.
- Try to convey enthusiasm and interest.
- Do not use slang or swear words.

A short history of car engines

Throughout the 19th century people had been experimenting with engines that might be able to power a motor vehicle, as it became clear that steam engines, while effective for railways, had major limitations for smaller vehicles.

Although the internal combustion engine was invented in 1806, the first practical motor vehicle was produced in 1885 by Karl Benz. The Benz Patent Motorwagen had a single-piston engine and generated two-thirds of one horsepower.

The first car manufacturers were French, among them Peugeot, who began production in 1891. Henry Ford in the US was the first to produce cars on an assembly line.

The Model T Ford was released in 1908 and by 1914 mass production made it the first affordable car. It had a 2.9 litre four-cylinder engine with 22 horsepower. By 1920 half of all the motor vehicles in the world were Model T Fords.

Over the last 125 years car engines have been continuously refined. Today they are quieter, less polluting and more fuel-efficient as well as more powerful and longer lasting. The following are some of the key moments in the evolution of engines.

- In 1890, Wilhelm Maybach produced a four-stroke engine. While this was more complex and more expensive to produce than earlier engines, it was much more fuel-efficient.

- In 1911, the Cadillac Motor Company introduced electric ignition and self-starting, which helped make starting easier.

- Fuel injection was first used on a large scale in the post-war period. It provides more power and increased fuel efficiency. However, it is also more complex and can result in more costly repairs.

- The lighter weight of aluminum engine blocks allowed more efficiency and better handling, though they can warp at high temperatures.

- Overhead camshafts led to better performance but also increased complexity.

- Clean diesels gave fuel economy and cleaner emissions but with a higher initial cost.

- Although some electric vehicles were produced at the start of the 20th century, hybrid engines have recently become more popular for their improved fuel economy and reduced emissions.

Other recent developments have included variable valve timing and on-board engine computers. It seems certain that developments will continue to meet the challenges of the future.

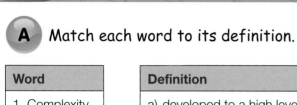

A Match each word to its definition.

Word	Definition
1 Complexity	a) developed to a high level of effectiveness or sophistication
2 Warp	b) the gradual development of something to a more complex and better form
3 Refined	c) being made up of many interrelated things
4 Evolution	d) to twist or bend out of shape

B Read the text and answer these questions.

1 When was the original Ford Model T introduced?

2 Write down three ways in which today's engines are better than those of the past.

a)

b)

c)

3 What kind of engine did the very first motor vehicle have?

4 What was the benefit of fuel injection?

5 Which improvement led to more efficiency and better handling?

C Put the following developments in chronological order:

The Model T Ford   Fuel injection   Four-stroke engines

The Benz Patent Motorwagen   The First Peugeot

1

2

3

4

5

D Early engine developments focused on increasing power and improving handling, while later ones have placed more emphasis on fuel economy.
Plan for a discussion about this statement. Consider the following questions:

- Do you agree or disagree with the statement? For what reasons?
- Which do you think is more important – more power or better fuel efficiency?
- Is there always a trade-off between power and economy?
- Is the focus on fuel economy being driven by the need for cheaper running costs or concern for the environment?
- What development do you think might be next?

Write notes about the points you will make.

E Tick the boxes for each improvement to show which has:

- resulted in higher costs
- improved fuel efficiency
- made the engine more complex.

For some of the improvements you will need to tick more than one box.

Improvement	Higher costs	Fuel efficiency	More complex
Four-stroke engines			
Overhead camshafts			
Clean diesels			
Fuel injection			

F   Refer to the text and insert a word in each gap so that the paragraph makes sense.

The first motor vehicle that the average person could [＿＿＿＿＿＿＿] to buy was the

Ford Model T. The [＿＿＿＿＿＿] had just 22 [＿＿＿＿＿＿], while the average

for a car engine today is nearer to 100. This has been the result of a continuous series

of [＿＿＿＿＿] to the internal [＿＿＿＿＿＿] engine. Developments such as

fuel [＿＿＿＿＿], clean [＿＿＿＿＿] and hybrid [＿＿＿＿＿＿] have

led to more [＿＿＿＿＿], better performance and improved [＿＿＿＿＿]

efficiency.

G   Some of the statements below are complete sentences, others are not. Underline the ones that are a complete sentence.

1   More fuel efficient.

2   The engines of today have more horsepower.

3   Lighter weight and better handling.

4   Fuel injection gives an engine more power.

5   Better fuel economy from hybrid engines.

6   Today's engines are more powerful, quieter and cause less pollution.

7   Do you think that engines are more fuel efficient today?

8   Overhead camshafts – better performance but more complex.

Rewrite the statements that are not sentences as full sentences.

FOCUS ON Active listening

Some people are described as 'good listeners'. When you think about someone who is good at conversation you may find that it is because they listen more than they speak. Being able to listen attentively and remember what people say is a valuable skill.

A How do you feel if someone you are talking to does the following things?

1 Interrupts you while you are speaking

2 Spends their time leafing through some papers

3 Yawns

4 Keeps looking at their watch

These are all examples of poor listening habits – they make us feel uncomfortable and ill at ease.

B How do you feel if someone you are talking to does the following things?

1 Looks at you kindly

2 Nods their head in agreement

3 Smiles

4 Asks you appropriate questions

These are examples of good listening habits – they make us feel more comfortable and 'listened to'.

We can all become better listeners by using what is known as 'active listening'. Active listening involves really paying attention to people when they speak, being interested in what they are saying, and showing that you are listening.

 Use this checklist to practise active listening skills.

Active listening checklist

- ☐ Do not try to do other things when you are meant to be listening.
- ☐ Sit or stand so that you can see the other person comfortably. Make sure there is enough space to hear each other clearly without crowding them.
- ☐ Use eye contact well – look at the other person regularly without staring at them.
- ☐ Use positive body language, such as leaning forward, smiling and using other facial expressions.
- ☐ Avoid things that show lack of interest or impatience, such as folded arms, yawning, tapping your fingers.
- ☐ Give the speaker time to think and organise their thoughts.
- ☐ Do not interrupt.
- ☐ Nod your head. Encourage with comments such as 'Yes' and 'I see'.
- ☐ Check your understanding of what the person has said from time to time. Say, 'So you mean ...?'
- ☐ Ask questions to show interest and to encourage the other person to continue.
- ☐ Make an effort to really *hear* what the person is trying to say. Avoid jumping to conclusions or judging people.

Practise using these techniques next time you listen to someone, whether one to one or in a group.

Three cars for just under £1,500

1999 Ford Focus

Ford Focus 1.6 – Silver hatchback, 1999. Manual, unleaded, alloy wheels, central locking, electric mirrors, electric windows, radio, airbags, 5-dr, 12 mths MOT, 3 mths tax, just been serviced, power steering, very clean and tidy inside and out, lady owner, selling due to my daughter buying new car and I'm having hers. £1,495.00.

1996 BMW 3 series

BMW 3 Series – Black saloon, 1996. Manual, unleaded, ABS, alarm, immobiliser, alloy wheels, CD player, central locking, electric mirrors, electric windows, power steering, radio, sunroof, airbags, climate control, parking sensor. This is a very nice example of the E46 model in black. It has good service history (BMW and others) and has been well cared for. 3 mths tax, tested until the end of Sept. It has an aftermarket (legal) powerflow exhaust fitted (original available) which sounds gorgeous. Used daily, it is extremely reliable. Comes with spare keys and extra interior mats. £1,490.00.

2002 Citroën Saxo

Citroën Saxo 1.1i Desire – Silver hatchback, 2002. Manual, unleaded, alarm, 3-dr, CD player, central locking, e/w, stereo radio, sunroof, airbags, tinted windows, 10 mths MOT, 6 mths tax, 2 owners, 78,000 mls, PAS, electric windows, excellent throughout, remote alarm, immobiliser, drives very nicely. £1,399.00 ono.

A What is the main purpose of the adverts in the text 'Three cars for just under £1,500'?

B What do the following abbreviations stand for?

Abbreviation	Stands for
1 mths	
2 PAS	
3 ABS	
4 dr	
5 ono	
6 e/w	

C Tick the box to show which feature is found on which car.

	Ford	BMW	Citroën
1 Saloon			
2 6 months tax			
3 ABS			
4 Tinted windows			
5 Recently serviced			
6 Mileage			
7 Powerflow exhaust			
8 Reason for selling			

D According to the text, which car may not have the following:

1 Alloy wheels

2 CD player

3 Immobiliser

4 Electric mirrors

E In your group, discuss the three adverts. You could make notes below.

- Which car do you think sounds most attractive?

- Only one advert gives a reason for selling. Do you think it is a problem that the others do not?

- Only one advert states the mileage. Do you think it is a problem that the others do not?

- Do you have any reservations about any of the adverts? Does anything sound too good to be true?

F Which car would you go to look at? Give three reasons.

Car chosen:

Reason 1

Reason 2

Reason 3

G Find a phrase in each description that is designed to persuade you to buy the car.

1 Ford

2 BMW

3 Citroën

H Read these three case studies.

Jalal is strapped for cash so wants to pay the least possible for a car. He listens to hip hop CDs whenever he drives. He would like tinted windows and an alarm.

Emma is keen on cars and happy to spend hours tinkering with them. She likes motorsports and is keen to fit additional features. She is keen on ABS and would prefer a saloon car.

Ben just wants a car to get around. He does not know the first thing about mechanics so wants something reliable. He does not want to waste time over the next few months worrying about the MOT test. He often gives people lifts so would prefer five doors.

I Which car would you recommend for each person? Write a short note to each one giving your recommendation and explaining why you think this car might suit them.

1 Jalal

2 Emma

3 Ben

Hazardous substances

People working in motor vehicle workshops and garages are exposed to substances that could harm their health. The term for these is 'hazardous substances'. They may include chemicals, dust, fumes, and so on.

The Control of Substances Hazardous to Health (COSHH) Regulations 2002 are there to protect workers' health in all industries. Employers have to:

- assess the risks of working with the hazardous substances
- eliminate or reduce these risks
- introduce measures to control the risks where it is not possible to eliminate them
- where necessary, monitor the health of employees.

If a COSHH risk assessment has been made, everyone has to follow its recommendations.

What are the risks?

Hazardous substances used in workshops and garages include exhaust fumes, fuels, oil, lubricants, solvents, batteries, asbestos in old brakes, as well as some cleaning and valeting materials and disinfectants.

Mixing and spraying paints falls under the COSHH Regulations because many paints and solvents give off flammable vapour that is hazardous to health if people breathe it in. Vehicle paint sprayers are 80 times more likely to get asthma than other workers. So it is important for employers to have clear procedures for storing, mixing and spraying paints (such as spray booths with good extraction) to reduce the risks.

Powered disc cutting and sanding creates large quantities of dust. Employers must keep dust to a minimum, minimise the number of people exposed to dust and provide protective equipment and changing areas.

The risk assessment

To carry out COSHH risk assessments, employers should think about how each substance is used and for what tasks. They should pay particular attention to any processes that produce dust, vapour, fumes or gas that people could breathe in. They should also look out for substances that come into contact with the skin such as dust or liquids.

Employers can then decide on the action they need to take to prevent or control exposure to hazardous substances. They should start with the substances that could cause most harm. If possible, use less-harmful products to decrease the risk. If products cannot be replaced, precautions should be taken, such as good ventilation and protective equipment.

The results of the assessment must be shared with employees.

A In a group, discuss these questions. You could write notes below.

- Have you heard of COSHH?

- Do you know a company that does risk assessments?

- Who does the risk assessment?

- What training about hazardous substances have you had?

B Match each word to its definition.

Word		Definition
1 Hazardous		a) can catch fire
2 Extraction		b) can harm living things or the environment
3 Eliminate		c) removing air, dust and fumes from an area
4 Flammable		d) to completely get rid of something

 C Choose two words from the table above and write them in a sentence.

1

2

D An important part of any group discussion is responding to what other people say. If someone said the following things to you about protecting health in the workplace, what would you say?

- You cannot just reply 'I agree' or 'I disagree'.

- You need to add something more to the discussion.

1 'It takes too long to do the COSHH paperwork. I do not have the time.'
What would you say?

2 'Motor technicians are able to look after themselves. They do not need a nanny state telling them how to stay healthy.'
What would you say?

3 'All garages are as bad as each other. None of them care about their workers' health and safety.'
What would you say?

4 'Motor technicians should take more care of their own health and safety, not leave it all to management.'
What would you say?

E Refer to the text and answer the following questions.

1 Define 'hazardous substance'.

2 Why is paint defined as a hazardous substance?

3 How can your employers minimise the risks from dust?

F With a partner, discuss a motor vehicle garage or workshop that you know.

1 Note down some of the hazardous substances they use.

2 How do they reduce the risks from hazardous substances?

Substance	How risk is reduced

G Draft a poster for a motor vehicle organisation that you know. The poster should be about the hidden dangers from hazardous substances.

FOCUS ON Quote marks

We use quote marks (also called 'speech marks') when we want to include words that somebody has said, as in these examples.

What time will we meet?

7.30 would be good.

That's great. See you then.

- 'What time will we meet?' asked Tom.
- Ruth replied, '7.30 would be good.'
- Tom said, 'That's great. See you then.'

The quote marks show which words are spoken, in much the same way as speech bubbles in a cartoon.

Note that if you start a sentence with 'Tom said' or similar you should put a comma before the quote.

When to use quote marks:

- Every time a new person speaks, start a new paragraph.
- Put quote marks at the start and at the end of the spoken text.
- Use either single (') or double (") quote marks, but be consistent.
- Start each quote with a capital letter.
- Include punctuation (e.g. the question mark above) within the quote marks.

A Copy these sentences, but insert quote marks and other punctuation.

1   Ruth asked Are you ready for lunch yet

2   My shift starts at nine o'clock said Ed

3   When do you finish work Yusuf asked

4   Emma said They will collect their car at four

If you have a piece of speech that is split into two parts, the punctuation is different. For example:

- 'That's great,' said Tom. 'See you then.'

Notice that:

- There are two sets of speech marks.
- There is a comma at the end of the first piece of speech.
- There is a full stop at the end of the second piece of speech.

B Copy these sentences, but insert quote marks and other punctuation.

1   The car has not been valeted yet said Priya You will be able to collect it at four o'clock.

2   Shall we take it for a test drive asked Mike It might help us to identify the problem.

Inverted commas

Just as we use quote marks (or 'inverted commas') to show words that someone has spoken, so we can use them to show:

- the title of a book or article
- an extract from a book, article or the internet that you include in your writing.

You can include short extracts within a paragraph, with inverted commas before and after each title or extract.

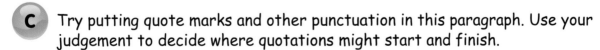

In the article 'Industry award for Motor Codes' the writer reports that the Motor Industry Code of Practice for Service and Repair 'has grown rapidly since it was set up in 2008, generating custom for subscribed garages'.

Longer extracts may need their own paragraph.

C Try putting quote marks and other punctuation in this paragraph. Use your judgement to decide where quotations might start and finish.

The article MOT research reveals worst performers states that European manufacturers are at the bottom of the table for first MOT failures. It points out that the worst performer, Renault, was followed by the British-built Mini with Citroën being third from bottom.

It goes on to say that the top 10 best-performing cars are from Japanese manufacturers.

 **You have passed your test – now what?**

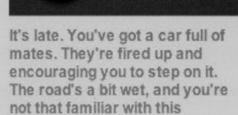

It's late. You've got a car full of mates. They're fired up and encouraging you to step on it. The road's a bit wet, and you're not that familiar with this stretch.

Now how good a driver are you really?

Momentum, the IAM assessment designed exclusively for under 26-year-old car drivers will help you find out.

So, you've passed your driving test and the last thing you want to think about is another test. You're a pretty good driver and you definitely don't need L plates any more but you know that sometimes you end up in situations where your driving skills are challenged. Maybe it's when you're on a night out with a car full of mates and it's your turn to be the designated driver. Everyone is fired up for the night and having a laugh but you know you still need to keep focused on the road as well as the banter. This is when Momentum steps in.

The results of the recent IAM report *Young Drivers – Where and When They are Unsafe* indicates that young drivers (aged 17–25) are the most vulnerable group on our roads and are the most at risk group of road users likely to be killed or seriously injured.

The following details are from the most recent Department for Transport report *Reported Road Accidents Involving Young Car Drivers: Great Britain* (published 03/02/2011)

- Of the 163,554 reported personal injury road accidents, over 42,000 (26%) involved at least one driver aged 17–24.
- 191 young drivers were killed (27% of all fatalities), 2,026 young drivers were killed or seriously injured (27% of all KSI casualties).
- 564 people were killed (25% of total road fatalities) as a result of a young driver car accident.
- Of the 2,026 young drivers involved in serious accidents, 71% were male.
- Nearly one-third of young drivers involved in accidents were aged 18–19.

Momentum is NOT a test

Step 1 – An online assessment that can be completed in the comfort of your own home prior to your on-road assessment date. It helps to assess the environment in which you typically drive and gets a handle on your attitude to road risks.

Step 2 – A 60-minute on-road, general assessment by a qualified IAM examiner. At the end of the drive you will receive a copy of the completed assessment form.

The result? You are more able to keep your focus and enjoy the journey, even if the pressure is on.

Momentum is only £40 and you can buy online by visiting our eshop – just click HERE

If you would like to purchase a gift voucher just click here.

Alternatively, click here to download the Momentum brochure, which also has an application form that you can complete and return to the IAM.

A Read the text and answer these questions.

1 Who is this text aimed at?

2 What is the main purpose of the text?

3 What is the brand name of the product?

4 How much does it cost?

B Choose the correct answer to the following questions.

1 Which drivers are most likely to be seriously injured on the roads?

   a) Drivers aged 20–26

   b) Young male drivers

   c) Drivers aged 17–25

2 Who can do the Momentum assessment?

   a) Any young learner driver

   b) Anyone under 26 who has passed their driving test

   c) Anyone who wants to improve their driving

3 How many accidents involved a driver aged between 17 and 24?

   a) 42,000

   b) 2,026

   c) 191

4 The text does not tell you what IAM stands for. What do you think is most likely?

   a) Independent Assessment Method

   b) Improve Anyone's Motoring

   c) Institute of Advanced Motorists

C With a partner, discuss the following aspects of the layout, features and tone of the advert.

Make a note of your response after each question.

1 What aspects of the look of the text tell you that it is from a website?

2 What design features are used to attract your attention?

3 The text is written to persuade young drivers to do the Momentum assessment. Give two ways in which it does this.

a) [   ]

b) [   ]

4 How does the style of writing show that it is aimed at young people?

5 The brand name 'Momentum' means developing and increasing power. Do you think this is a good name? Give a reason for your answer.

Share your answers with the rest of the group.

D Write answers to these questions.

1 What are the two ways that you can apply to buy Momentum?

a) [   ]

b) [   ]

2 What are the two parts of the assessment?

a) [   ]

b) [   ]

3 The website says you can buy a gift voucher. Who might be interested in this?

[   ]

E Choose a word from those given below that means the same as a word in the list.

before   shows   friends   chat   buy

1 Banter [   ]

2 Mates [   ]

3 Indicates [   ]

4 Purchase [   ]

5 Prior [   ]

F Write an email to a friend telling them about Momentum and how they can get more information.

From:

To:

Subject:

Working time and mimimum wage

If you are under 18 but over school-leaving age you are classed as a young worker. You reach school-leaving age at the end of the summer term of the school year in which you turn 16.

Working time limits

A young worker cannot usually be made to work more than eight hours per day or 40 hours per week. These hours cannot be averaged over a longer period and you are not allowed to ignore these restrictions.

You'll only be able to work longer hours if you need to:

- keep the continuity of service or production, or
- respond to a surge in demand for a service or product.

This is provided that:

- there is no adult available to do the work, and
- your training needs are not negatively affected.

The minimum wage

You become eligible for the national minimum wage (NMW) when you're older than school-leaving age. The rate of NMW will then depend on your exact age. There isn't a national minimum wage for people under 16.

There are different levels of NMW, depending on your age and whether you are an apprentice. The rates from 1 October 2012 are:

- £6.19 per hour – the main rate for workers aged 21 and over
- £4.98 per hour – the 18–20 rate
- £3.68 per hour – the 16–17 rate for workers above school-leaving age but under 18.

The apprentice rate is £2.65 per hour for apprentices under 19, or for those aged 19 or over and in the first year of their apprenticeship.

Most workers in the UK over school-leaving age are legally entitled to be paid at least the NMW and all employers have to pay it to you if you are entitled to it. It makes no difference:

- if you are paid weekly or monthly, by cheque, in cash or in another way
- if you work full time, part time or any other working pattern
- if you work at your employer's own premises or elsewhere
- what size your employer is
- where you work in the UK.

You are entitled to the NMW even if you sign a contract agreeing to be paid at a lower rate. This is regardless of whether you sign of your own free will or because your employer persuades or makes you – you must still be paid the proper rate.

The Pay and Work Rights Helpline gives confidential help and advice on the NMW. If you need to work longer than 40 hours a week or you think your employer is unfairly asking you to work over this limit, you can call them on 0800 917 2368. The helpline can take calls in over 100 languages.

A Read the text and answer the questions.

1 What does NMW stand for?

2 What is the NMW for people aged 18–20?

3 Who can you call for help and advice about the NMW?

4 What is the maximum time each day that a young worker can be made to work for?

5 In what circumstances can a young worker be asked to exceed the working time limit?

6 When does a young person reach school-leaving age?

B True or false?

Which of these statements are true and which are false?

1 The Pay and Work Rights Helpline will tell your employer that you contacted them.　　True ◯　　False ◯

2 A young worker cannot normally be made to work more than 40 hours a week.　　True ◯　　False ◯

3 The NMW does not apply to you if you are paid in cash.　　True ◯　　False ◯

4 An apprentice aged 25 and in their first year is entitled to a NMW of £2.65 per hour.　　True ◯　　False ◯

5 A young worker will be under 18 years old.　　True ◯　　False ◯

6 All workers above school-leaving age in the UK are entitled to a NMW of at least £4.98 per hour.　　True ◯　　False ◯

C Insert a word from the list below into the text so that it makes sense.

minimum   hour   opposed   jobs   increase

The national [＿＿＿＿＿＿] wage was introduced in the UK in 1999 when it was set

at £3.60 per [＿＿＿＿＿＿]. People who [＿＿＿＿＿＿] the NMW said that it

would reduce the number of [＿＿＿＿＿＿] and [＿＿＿＿＿＿] inflation, but

that did not happen.

D Write a sentence to answer each of the following questions. Make sure you use capital letters and full stops where they are needed.

1 Do small employers have to pay the NMW?

2 I am from Romania and my English is not very good. Will the helpline understand me?

3 My employer made me sign a contract to be paid £2.50 an hour. Does that mean I am not entitled to the NMW?

E Discuss wages and working hours in your group.

- Do staff in garages and workshops work long hours?
- Do you think that motor vehicle workers are well paid?
- Why do people choose to work in the motor vehicle sector?
- What do you know about trade unions? How do they help? Would you join one?

F Read about the person below.

I am an apprentice in a repair workshop. A lot of the other people there work a 50- or 60-hour week. My manager says I must do the same as it is normal in our sector and our customers expect work to be done on time. I am only given the rubbish jobs to do, such as clearing up and making coffee – I am not learning anything. I also miss my off-job training days sometimes. It is making me really tired and I am struggling to complete my portfolio.

What advice would you give this person?

G Choose the correct answer to each of these questions.

1 The NMW for workers over 21 is:

a) £4.98

b) £6.19

c) £3.68

2 The NMW does not apply to:

a) people paid a monthly salary

b) people under 16

c) people who agree to a lower rate.

3 The Pay and Work Rights Helpline gives advice on:

a) contracts of employment

b) health and safety at work

c) working time limits.

H Draft a leaflet for apprentices aged 16–19 telling them about their rights.

FOCUS ON Preparing a talk

You may be asked to give a talk or presentation, either as part of your course or at work. To do this well, you need to consider four key elements:

- planning
- using visual aids
- rehearsing or practising
- getting feedback.

Planning

Start by identifying a topic or subject for your presentation and then think about the purpose and audience.

- Purpose: Is your presentation intended to *inform, persuade* or *advise*?
- Audience: What do they already know? What *language* and *style* is appropriate?

A presentation must have a clear structure. It should start with a general introduction telling people what the talk is about and end with a summary of what you have said.

You should then identify the main sections. For a 10-minute presentation you should have three to five main headings, organised in a logical order.

A Here are the main headings for a talk about how a motor vehicle organisation handles complaints. Organise them into a logical sequence.

1 Examples of complaints

2 Summary

3 Listening to a complaint

4 Company or organisation procedures

5 Introduction

6 How complaints are resolved

Once you have identified your main headings, you can add details of what you will say under each one.

For example, under 'Listening to a complaint' your plan may include the following points.

- Be respectful and courteous.
- Find somewhere private to talk so that you can maintain confidentiality.
- Listen carefully to the individual and be aware of your body language.
- Keep calm and speak quietly to help the person relax.
- Acknowledge the complaint so that they know they have been heard.
- Do not pre-judge the situation or offer your own opinion.
- Tell the person what will happen next.

B How will you plan the outline of your talk? Tick the one that would suit you best.

◯ Brainstorm all of your ideas on the topic and then organise them in order.

◯ Use a mind map to organise your ideas.

◯ Write a list and then reorganise it.

◯ Use a 'storyboard' format similar to that used for a film or video.

Using visual aids

Relevant images and visual aids can really bring a presentation to life. They can include:

- images, such as photographs, diagrams and paintings
- a model or other physical object or a wall display
- PowerPoint, whiteboard or flipchart.

If you use PowerPoint you can incorporate diagrams and pictures. Be careful not to put too many words on a slide or people will be reading it rather than listening to you.

Cue cards

Cue cards will help you when you are giving your presentation. They:

- are easy to hold and avoid you having pages of notes
- remind you of your main points through key words or phrases
- will not distract your audience as much as big sheets of paper.

Here are some tips for writing cue cards:

- Use cards about the size of a filing card (15 cm × 10 cm).
- Write one key word or phrase for the main heading.
- Write no more than four more detailed points and number them.
- Write in large letters or capitals.
- Number your cards in case you drop them!

C How will you practise your talk?

It is very important to practise your presentation before you do it for real. Think of it in the same way as a rehearsal for a performance. This will help with the content and with aspects of delivery, such as tone, pitch of voice and speed.

Decide whether you will practise on your own in front of a mirror or by recording yourself, with a friend or with your tutor, or in front of a small group.

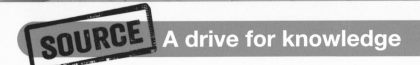

The **driving theory test** explained

The theory test is made up of two parts – multiple choice and hazard perception. You need to pass both parts to pass the theory test.

If you pass one part and fail the other, you will fail the whole test and you will need to take both parts again.

The multiple-choice part

Before the test starts you will be given instructions on how it works.

You can choose to do a practice session to get used to the layout of the test. At the end of the practice session, the real test will begin. Here is how it works:

- A question and several possible answers will appear on a computer screen – you have to select the correct answer. Some questions may need more than one answer.
- You can move between questions and 'flag' questions that you want to come back to later in the test.

Some car and motorcycle questions will be given as a case study. The case study will:

- show a short story that five questions will be based on
- focus on real-life examples and experiences that you could come across when driving.

The hazard perception part

Before you start the hazard perception part, you will be shown a short video clip about how it works. You will then be shown a series of video clips on a computer screen. The clips:

- feature everyday road scenes
- contain at least one developing hazard – but one of the clips will feature two developing hazards.

How the hazard perception scoring works

The earlier you notice a developing hazard and make a response, the higher you will score. The most you can score for each developing hazard is five points.

To get a high score you need to:

- respond to the developing hazard during the early part of its development
- press the mouse button as soon as you see a hazard developing.

You will not be able to review your answers to the hazard perception test.

If you click continuously or in a pattern during a clip a message will appear at the end. It will tell you that you have scored zero for that particular clip.

A True or false?

Which of these statements are true and which are false, according to the text?

1 If you fail the hazard perception part of the test, you only need to take that part again?   True ◯   False ◯

2 You can do a practice session to get used to the multiple-choice test.   True ◯   False ◯

3 The test is done on a computer.   True ◯   False ◯

4 There are three questions in the hazard perception part of the test.   True ◯   False ◯

5 The multiple-choice test includes case studies.   True ◯   False ◯

B Read the text and answer these questions.

1 What should you do if you want to pass a question and go back to it later?

2 How should you answer multiple-choice questions?

3 How do you get a high score on the hazard perception part?

4 What is the highest score you can get for a question about a developing hazard?

5 What is the case study based on?

C The statements below are not complete sentences. Rewrite them, adding the correct punctuation, to make them proper sentences.

1 video clips contain hazards

2 five points for each hazard

3 do a practice session

D Write down what each of these words means.

1	Hazard	
2	Perception	
3	Response	

E Some of your group will have taken the driving theory test already. Get into small groups that include one of these people.

- The person who has taken the test should describe what it was like and give tips about how to prepare for it.

- The others should make notes about the important points.

F Write a short note to a friend who is about to take their driving theory test. Explain what the test is like and give them two pieces of advice.

G Read the text and choose the correct answer to each question below.

From:

To:

Subject: **Theory test experience**

The test centre was really easy to find. When I went in, someone told me to take a seat. I handed over my provisional driving licence – you have to take the photocard and paper one or you will not be allowed to sit the test. I was given a key to a locker to put all my belongings in. You are not allowed to go into the test room with anything other than the locker key.

The lady guarding the test room asks to make sure you are not smuggling anything in, but my jeans were skintight so there was no chance of me hiding anything.

There were quite a lot of people already in the test room in the middle of their exam. It made me feel like I was late for school. You sit at a computer in an individual booth and then the test begins. You have 57 minutes to do the test but you can leave if you finish earlier. Sally

1   What can you take into the test room with you?

   a)   Locker key and driving licence

   b)   Phone and locker key

   c)   Locker key only

2   What ID do you need to take with you?

   a)   Both parts of your provisional licence

   b)   Provisional licence and passport

   c)   Your photocard driving licence

3   In the test room:

   a)   everyone starts the test at the same time

   b)   you start when you sit down

   c)   you cannot leave until everyone else has finished.

4   How did Sally feel when she went into the test room?

   a)   Nervous

   b)   Like being at school

   c)   Like being late for school

 **Alternative fuels**

New power in the tank

Conventional vehicles run on petrol or diesel, both of which are fossil fuels. Although these have served us well for over a century, there are two significant problems with them. They are non-renewable, which means we will eventually run out of them, and they produce substantial emissions of greenhouse gases, responsible for global warming.

Of the two fuels, diesel produces slightly fewer emissions and better fuel efficiency.

Several alternative fuels are available commercially at the moment. These include the following.

Liquid petroleum gas (LPG)

LPG is a gas stored in liquid form under pressure. It produces fewer emissions than conventional fuels. LPG powers the car in much the same way as conventional fuel and most LPG cars are dual fuel, with both an LPG cylinder and a petrol tank.

Biofuel

Biofuel (usually biodiesel) is fuel produced from renewable sources – many plant and animal fats can be used to create a biofuel. Vehicles need to be converted to use biofuel. Biofuels also produce fewer emissions, but they require extensive agricultural land.

Electricity

Electric cars use large (usually lithium) battery units to power one or two large AC motors. They need recharging, usually every 50–100 miles. A full charge will take about six hours, but it is possible to get an 80 per cent charge in 30–40 minutes.

Hybrid

Hybrid cars use a mix of conventional fuel – usually petrol, but diesel models are being produced – and electricity.

- In **parallel hybrids** the car can be powered by both a fuel engine and an electric motor.
- In **series hybrids** the car is only powered by the electric motor – the fuel engine does not drive the car, it generates electricity for the motor.

Fuel cell

Fuel cells combine hydrogen and oxygen to produce electricity to drive an electric motor. They offer potential benefits in terms of renewable energy and reduced emissions. However, fuel cell technology is in its early stages at the moment and in the UK it is mainly found in a limited number of London taxis and buses.

Summary

Each type of alternative fuel allows the vehicle to use less fossil fuel than a conventional vehicle. For example, while a Toyota Auris petrol model will produce 135–150 g/km of CO_2, a diesel model will produce 128 g/km and a petrol hybrid will produce around 90 g/km. A hybrid can also give better fuel efficiency than a conventional car.

A Read the text and choose the correct answer to each question.

1 Which of these best describes LPG?

    a) A fuel produced from renewable sources such as rapeseed ◯

    b) A gas stored in liquid form under pressure ◯

    c) A way of combining hydrogen and oxygen to produce electricity ◯

2 How long is it likely to take to fully charge an electric car?

    a) 30 minutes ◯

    b) 40 minutes ◯

    c) Six hours ◯

3 Which of these best describes a series hybrid?

    a) The car is powered by both a fuel engine and an electric motor ◯

    b) The car is powered by the fuel engine only ◯

    c) The car is powered by the electric motor only ◯

4 Which of these best describes a parallel hybrid?

    a) The car is powered by both a fuel engine and an electric motor ◯

    b) The car is powered by the fuel engine only ◯

    c) The car is powered by the electric motor only ◯

B Write down answers to these questions.

1 What are the two problems with fossil fuels?

a)

b)

2 According to the text, what is a disadvantage of biofuels?

3 How far does the text say an electric car can go before it will need recharging?

4 What does the text say are the potential benefits of fuel cells?

C In your group, discuss these questions. You could make notes below.

- Have you had any experience of using or working with any cars powered by the alternative fuels described?

- Which of the options described are most promising for the future?

- Are you aware of other possible alternatives to fossil fuels?

D An important part of any group discussion is responding to what other people say. If someone said the following things to you about alternative fuels, what would you say?

- You cannot just reply 'I agree' or 'I disagree'.
- You need to add something more to the discussion.

1 'No alternative fuel is ever going to work as well as petrol or diesel.'
   What would you say?

2 'We have enough fossil fuels for the next few decades. Why should we worry about running out of them?'
   What would you say?

3 'The planet is warming too fast. We need to stop using fossil fuels straight away.'
   What would you say?

E A member of your family would like your advice about alternative fuels. They are planning to change their car and they are concerned both about the increasing cost of petrol and diesel, and the impact on global warming. They drive 8,000–10,000 miles a year, mainly short journeys in and near the town where they live. However, they like to take the car on holiday as well. You need to write to them setting out the options, drawing on the text and your own knowledge. With a partner, make a plan for what you will write. Make notes for four paragraphs as follows:

1 An introductory paragraph introducing the main options.

2 Advantages of each type of fuel.

3 Disadvantages of each type of fuel.

4 A conclusion where you recommend which option(s) you think may suit them best.

F Produce a first draft of your four paragraphs and discuss it with a partner.

FOCUS ON Writing good paragraphs

Paragraphs are important in all pieces of writing that are more than a few sentences long. They provide a clear structure to longer emails, letters, assignments and reports. Good paragraphs divide up the text and separate out the main ideas. They make it easier for the reader to follow your argument.

The principles for writing good paragraphs are as follows:

- Use a new paragraph for each new idea.

- A paragraph can have just one or two sentences, though usually they will have three to six sentences.

- Each paragraph begins with the topic sentence, which introduces the idea.

- The other sentences then provide more information about this idea.

- All of the sentences should be relevant to the main idea.

Look at the first paragraph on this page. The topic sentence is the one beginning 'Paragraphs are important in'. The other sentences explain why they are important. There are four sentences altogether.

 A Read the following paragraph.

> There are different types of paragraph. You begin your piece of writing with an introductory paragraph, which introduces what you will write and why you are writing it. You then have one paragraph for each of the main ideas. You end with a concluding paragraph, which sums up what you have said.

Which is the topic sentence? How many other sentences are there?

Punctuating paragraphs

You punctuate paragraphs like this:

- Begin a new paragraph with a new line.

- Either leave a line space before the new paragraph, or indent the first line of the paragraph.

- Each sentence begins with a capital letter and ends with a full stop (or a question mark or exclamation mark).

B Turn the information about punctuating paragraphs on the previous page into a paragraph rather than a bullet list. You can use the same words, though you may want to make a few minor changes so that the paragraph reads better. Make sure you begin with a good topic sentence.

Introducing the paragraph

As we have seen, the first sentence is likely to be the topic sentence and will introduce the idea in the paragraph. Where possible, it is good to link back to what has gone before. You can do this with phrases like 'as we have seen', 'on the other hand' or 'however'. Try to make the topic sentence as interesting as possible.

Developing the paragraph

The other sentences will develop the idea in the topic sentence. They can do this in several ways, such as:

- explaining the idea in greater detail
- providing a list (like this one!)
- giving an example
- including some facts or figures.

However, the sentences must all be relevant to the topic and should not introduce a new idea.

Ending the paragraph

The final sentence may simply round off the paragraph. In some cases it may sum up what you have said or look forward to the next paragraph.

 C Turn these words and phrases into a paragraph about the role of a motor vehicle engineer.

motor vehicle engineer   changing role   modern cars   technology   safety

fuel efficiency   more computer-controlled systems   not just mechanical expertise

D Next time you need to draft a paragraph, use this checklist to check what you have written.

- ◯ Does the paragraph start a new line?
- ◯ Is there a clear topic sentence?
- ◯ Do other sentences develop the main idea?
- ◯ Are all sentences relevant to the main idea?
- ◯ Is the paragraph interesting?
- ◯ Is the punctuation correct?

Tyre types

There are several different types of tyre that you can buy for your car. What you choose depends on what you use your car for, where you live and how you like the ride of your car.

Performance tyres or summer tyres

Performance tyres are designed for faster cars or for people who prefer to drive harder than the average consumer. They typically put performance and grip ahead of longevity by using a softer rubber compound. The tread block design favours outright grip rather than the ability to pump water out of the way on a wet road. The extreme examples of performance tyres are 'slicks' used in motor racing, which have no tread at all.

All-round or all-season tyres

These tyres are what you'll typically find on every production car that comes out of a factory. They're designed to be a compromise between grip, performance, longevity, noise and wet-weather safety. For increased tyre life, they are made with a harder rubber compound. The tyre should not be too noisy in normal use but should work fairly well in downpours and on wet roads.

Wet-weather tyres

Wet-weather tyres use a softer compound than performance tyres. The rubber needs to heat up more quickly in cold or wet conditions and needs to have as much mechanical grip as possible. The tread pattern moves water away quickly to keep the rubber in contact with the road surface.

Winter tyres

Winter tyres come at the other end of the spectrum to performance tyres. They are designed to work well in wintery conditions with snow and ice on the roads. Winter tyres typically have larger tread block patterns, while true snow tyres have tiny metal studs that bite into the snow and ice. The downside of this is that they are incredibly noisy on dry roads and wear out both the tyre and the road surface extremely quickly.

All-terrain tyres

All-terrain tyres are typically used on four-wheel drives and light trucks. They are larger tyres with stiff sidewalls and large tread block patterns that grip loose sand and dirt very well when off-road. The larger tread block means the tyres are very noisy on normal roads.

Mud tyres

At the extreme end of the all-terrain tyre classification are mud tyres. These have massive, super-chunky tread blocks that reduce slide and stopping distance in muddy conditions. They are hard-wearing, but they are not designed for use on normal roads.

A Match each word to its definition.

Word	Definition
1 Compromise	a) how long a tyre will last for
2 Longevity	b) a mix of different substances
3 Performance	c) a balance between different demands
4 Compound	d) the physical features of a piece of land
5 Terrain	e) the capabilities of a product

B According to the text, which of these types of tyre uses the softest rubber compound?

1 Performance tyres ◯

2 All-season tyres ◯

3 Wet-weather tyres ◯

C According to the text, which of these types of tyre is a compromise between grip, performance, longevity, noise and wet-weather safety?

1 Performance tyres ◯

2 All-season tyres ◯

3 Wet-weather tyres ◯

D According to the text, identify two types of tyre that are designed for off-road use.

1 [   ]

2 [   ]

E Match the tyre to the appropriate feature.
Which tyre has each of these features?

Tyre	Feature
1 All-terrain tyres	a) tiny metal studs
2 Snow tyres	b) put performance and grip ahead of longevity
3 Performance tyres	c) reduce slide and stopping distance
4 Mud tyres	d) have no tread at all
5 Slick tyres	e) grip loose sand and dirt

F Which tyres would you prefer to use on your car? Give three reasons.

Tyre chosen:

Reason 1

Reason 2

Reason 3

G Share your answers to question F with a partner.

• Were your choices and reasons similar or different?

• Would your choices change in different circumstances?

• What tyres would you recommend to your friends?

H You recently used Mobile Tyres 4 U and were so pleased with the service you received that you would like to recommend them to a friend.

Mobile Tyres 4 U

Are you looking for cheap tyres for your car, van or caravan? Do you want high-performance or sports car tyres? We offer a wide range of winter tyres, all-terrain tyres, run-flat tyres and budget

tyres. We stock all of the major brand names, such as Pirelli, Bridgestone, Continental, Dunlop, Goodyear and Michelin, as well as mid-range products from companies, such as like Maxxis and GT Radial.

Our We Come 2 U service means you no longer need to take your car to a garage to change your tyres. We can come to you at home or work. We have mobile tyre fitters across the region. And if you're not sure which type of tyre is right for you, we can give you the best advice.

Call us now on 0800 123 4567 or email andy@mobiletyres4u. co.uk to book your personal tyre fitter.

Write an email to your friend explaining why Mobile Tyres 4 U are a good company to use.

From: you@youremail.co.uk

To: yourfriend@yourfriendsemail.co.uk

Subject: Mobile Tyres 4 U

Wales Rally GB

Wales Rally GB is Britain's round of the World Rally Championship. The GB Rally has been run 67 times since it started in 1932. Cardiff has hosted the Rally since 2000.

This year there will be a ceremonial start in Llandudno in North Wales on Thursday, 13 September. There will also be an autograph signing session featuring top international drivers, as well as demonstrations and displays.

The order in which competitors start the rally is seeded according to their world championship position. After each leg the competitors are re-seeded according to their overall position.

It will finish in Cardiff on 16 September. The official finish ceremony of the event will take place in Cardiff Bay after the final stage.

The Welsh Government has been the main funding partner since 2003. First Minister Carwyn Jones said: 'Wales Rally GB is a world-class sporting event that will provide a welcome boost for retailers, hotels and tourism operators. The rally is an ideal platform for Wales, showing a global audience what we have to offer.'

Iwan Davies, Chief Executive, Conwy County Borough Council said:

'We are really pleased to be hosting the start of WRGB again this year. Last year's event was a great success and I know that rally fans will be pleased to see the event starting in North Wales again, so we're preparing for another high turnout.'

The Rally relies on the assistance of almost 4,500 marshals over the three days. They are there to help ensure the safety of the spectators.

To celebrate the 80th anniversary, this year there will be a limited-edition 'Gold' pass that provides

spectators access to all stages, car parks, the qualifying test and service areas. The pass comes with its own unique gold lanyard, an exclusive key ring and a complimentary copy of the 80th anniversary DVD, which tells the history of the event. The cost of the Gold Rally Pass is £130, which is cheaper than buying tickets individually. Day tickets are available for £20, while tickets to Wednesday's qualifying stage are priced at £15 in advance. The start and finish ceremonies are free of charge.

A Read the text and answer these questions.

1 In which year did the GB Rally start?

2 Where will the Rally start this year?

3 Name two things that will feature in the ceremonial start.

a)

b)

4 How is the order in which competitors start decided?

5 What is the role of the marshalls?

6 Where will the race finish?

7 Who provides the main funding for Wales Rally GB?

B Match the quote to the person who said it.

Quote
1 'We're preparing for another high turnout'
2 'Wales Rally GB ... will provide a welcome boost for retailers'
3 'The rally is an ideal platform for Wales'
4 'Last year's event was a great success'

Person
a) Carwyn Jones
b) Iwan Davies
c) Chief Executive of Conwy Borough Council
d) Welsh First Minister

C Write down the type of ticket or pass you can get for each price.

1 £15

2 £20

3 £130

4 Free

D Write an email to a friend inviting them to join you for the finish ceremony of the Wales Rally GB. Tell them the date, where it will be held and how much the tickets cost.

From:

To:

Subject:

E Read the text below.

Rally terms

Clerk of the course: The official who is in control of the running of the Rally.

Flying finish: The flying finish marks the end of the stage – the cars cross it at full speed.

OTL (over time limit): Crews have to adhere to a timetable during the event, and arriving more than 15 minutes late at any one control or 30 minutes in total means they are OTL and out of the Rally.

Penalty: If crews arrive late at a control they are given a time penalty of 10 seconds for every minute or fraction of a minute they are late.

Road book: The road book contains maps, tulip diagrams and timings for all the special stages and road sections of the Rally.

Road section: The public roads that are used by the crews to drive between stages; these are not timed and crews must follow all road traffic laws.

Tulip diagrams: Diagrams in the road book to indicate which direction the crew should take at junctions. Introduced by the Tulip Rally in the 1950s.

Which of these statements are true and which are false, according to the text?

1 The flying finish marks the end of the Rally. True ⬭ False ⬭

2 Tulip diagrams give the crew directions. True ⬭ False ⬭

3 If a crew arrives at a control 20 minutes late, they will have to leave the Rally. True ⬭ False ⬭

4 Competitors can drive at any speed they like during the whole of the Rally. True ⬭ False ⬭

5 Marshals are in charge of the running of the Rally. True ⬭ False ⬭

F Add the correct punctuation and capital letters to the text below.

the official road book provides crews with maps diagrams and timings for the

wales rally gb tulip diagrams introduced by the tulip rally in the 1950s tell the

crews which direction to take at junctions

G You have received an invitation from a friend by text. Write it out again using whole words and punctuation.

Hey wubu2 cn u cum 2 mine 4 pty on sat @ 9 tb pls

FOCUS ON Conjunctions and prepositions

You can use conjunctions to join two simple sentences together to make a longer, more interesting sentence. For example:

- 'Mr Andrews prefers an automatic' is a simple sentence.

- 'He has arthritis' is also a simple sentence.

By joining them together with a conjunction we can make the sentence:

- 'Mr Andrews prefers an automatic **because** he has arthritis.'

A Choose from the common conjunctions below to join the following sentences together. In most cases there will be more than one option.

| and | so | but | because | or | though | as |

1 I like driving diesels. They can be a little less responsive.

2 Store flammable liquids in a safe place. They can cause fire or explosion.

3 We ask customers to bring their cars in before 9am. They can be ready for collection by lunchtime.

4 Lewis Hamilton's driving style has won him many fans. His celebrity lifestyle also keeps him in the gossip columns.

5 Toyota has led the industry in hybrids. Most other manufacturers are now developing hybrid models.

6 Many customers prefer the diesel version. It has lower CO_2 emissions and better fuel economy.

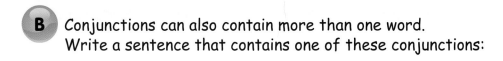

B Conjunctions can also contain more than one word.
Write a sentence that contains one of these conjunctions:

provided that   as long as

Prepositions

You may not know the grammatical term 'preposition' but you will recognise these words and probably know how to use them. A preposition links nouns, pronouns and phrases to other words in a sentence.

C Choose from the prepositions below to fill the gaps in each sentence.

with   about   to   of   for   from

1   The new model is very popular [   ] our customers.

2   We were all very sad [   ] Mr Singh's illness.

3   Jackie only eats free-range eggs because she is opposed [   ] factory farming.

4   I was not aware [   ] the health risks associated [   ] paint sprays.

5   Now I have been promoted I am responsible [   ] the induction [   ] new staff.

6   This workshop is completely different [   ] the one I was at before.

7   Off-the-job training is vital [   ] understanding the new developments in motor vehicle technology.

8   Working in a workshop in Scotland is similar [   ] doing the same job in England.

FOCUS ON Writing an email

You may use email to keep in touch with friends or family – these are **informal** emails. Sometimes, however, you will have to write a **formal** email.

Formal emails are anything to do with your professional work, such as an email to a client or to another person you have to liaise with in the motor vehicle industry. They also include emails relating to job applications or official organisations.

The tips below are very important for formal emails, but many of them apply to informal emails as well.

Top tips for writing effective emails

- Make sure you include something in the subject line. You would be amazed how many people forget to do this. If you are replying to an email you have received it may be all right to just keep the subject that is already there, but you need to decide whether you should change it.

- Write a clear and meaningful subject line. People often look at the subject line to decide whether to open or delete a message. Make sure the subject accurately describes the content. Do not put 'Important! Read Immediately' or 'Questions'.

- Think about how you will start the email. Although an email is more informal than a letter, if you are writing to someone for the first time and you do not know them, you should still write 'Dear xxx', not 'Hi'.

- Keep your message focused and readable. If you are making a number of points, separate them with bullets, dashes or paragraphs.

- Use standard spelling and avoid shortening words as you might in a text message.

- Only use capitals where you should for correct grammar. Writing all in capitals can come across as SHOUTING!

- Even if you are complaining or angry about something, be polite. Harsh words can sound much ruder in an email.

- If you are writing to someone you do not know, include your full name and any other information they may need, such as a contact telephone number.

- Think about how you will end your email. In a formal letter you might write 'Yours sincerely' or 'Yours faithfully', but it has become common practice in email to end politely with 'Best regards' or 'Kind regards'.

- Read your email carefully before you send it. First read it to see how it sounds – is the tone of voice right?

- Proofread your email for spelling mistakes or typos. Email may be a fast form of communication but that does not mean it should be rushed.

A Look at the email below.
Can you spot any mistakes? How could it be improved?

From:	JanetJ@thegarage.co.uk
Subject:	Problem
Date:	22 August 2012 10:31:45
To:	info@vehiclesupplies.co.uk

We are not happy with the brake linings you sent us. Their too thin and our customers keep havng accidents. Which makes them very distressed. Weve been using your company for ages and haven't had any problems before so why are we having them now? Are you using cheaper materail or a different supplier. What are you going to do about it.

From

Janet Jones

B Can you think of times when you have had to write a formal email?
Share your examples in the group.

C Draft an email in reply to this job advert. Use the checklist of tips to help you, and check your draft when you have finished.

Vacancy for motor vehicle technician

We are looking for a fully qualified technician with a strong technical knowledge and background. Experience of a car dealership would be useful but not essential. Qualifications and full UK driving licence essential. For further details and to apply please email Jill West at jwest@northgarages.co.uk

From:	
Subject:	
Date:	
To:	

FOCUS ON Writing a formal letter

Formal letters include letters that you write in your work, letters for job applications, letters of complaint, and so on. When you write formal letters you include these required elements:

- Your own address or the name, address and phone number of your organisation go at the top of the letter. Many organisations use headed paper so there is no need to type in the address.

- The name and address of the person you are writing to go next, on the left-hand side of the page, followed by the date.

- The 'salutation' comes next, which can be Dear Sir/Madam, Dear Mr/Mrs [surname] or Dear [first name] if you know the person well.

- It is then common to include the subject of the letter, or a reference (e.g. 'Re your letter of 5 May 2010').

- You then write the letter, broken into paragraphs.

- If you greeted the recipient by name, you should finish the letter with 'Yours sincerely' followed by your signature and name. If you began with 'Dear Sir/Madam' you should end with 'Yours faithfully'.

North Garages
Park Crescent
Manchester M23 4LS
Phone: 0161 123 4567

Mr Ben Simmons
Horley Tyres
25 Hincham Lane
Manchester M23 1LB

16 May 2012

Dear Mr Simmons

Tyre supplies

I am writing to express our thanks for supplying us with winter snow and ice tyres at short notice. These helped us to meet our customers' needs during the recent bad weather.

We would like to set up a preferred supplier arrangement with your company and I would be grateful if you could let me know the terms on which this could be arranged.

I look forward to hearing from you.

Yours sincerely

David Lawton
David Lawton, Service Manager

A Put the required elements of a formal letter in the correct order from the top of the page to the bottom by numbering each point.

- Your address ◯
- Your name and/or position ◯
- Subject of the letter or reference ◯
- Your signature ◯
- The correct closing phrase (Yours ...) ◯
- The date ◯
- The name and address of the person you are writing to ◯
- The salutation (Dear ...) ◯

Structure of the letter

The main content of the letter is likely to include:

- an introductory paragraph – this may thank the reader for an earlier letter or introduce you and explain why you are writing

- main paragraph(s) – these will set out the point(s) you want to make. Each point should have its own paragraph

- closing paragraph – you may end by summing up what you have said, proposing next steps, or saying 'I look forward to hearing from you'

Always use formal language, avoiding slang, abbreviations, and so on.

Checking what you have written

B Next time you write a formal letter, use this checklist:

- Have you included all of the required elements (names, addresses, date, salutation and closing elements)?
- Have you used headed paper if available?
- Is the reason you are writing clear?
- Is the tone of writing polite and professional?
- Have you used appropriate language?
- Have you explained why you are writing?
- Does each main point or idea have its own paragraph?
- Is everything easy to understand?
- Is it clear what will happen next?
- Are spelling, punctuation and grammar correct?